To Kurt, Paul and Andy,
who missed all the fun, I offer this
somewhat musty souvenir of Treasure Island
in the fatherly hope that, like my old tuxedo,
my navy shoes and certain other items of my hilarious
antique wardrobe, it will prove to have some
enduring interest to the new generation.

When I was a boy they built an island in the center of San Francisco Bay that was the capsule of my dreams. It was a peaceable island, crowned with towers and glittering with light, that seemed to float like a vision in a sea of gold — an earthly paradise where boys could feast on buttered scones and fried potatoes and the world was flat.

Officially, this bower of bliss was called the Golden Gate International Exposition, a forgettable name that scarcely anyone used and no one liked. We called it Treasure Island. For 372 days in 1939 and 1940 it gave refreshment to our lives, providing an interlude of consolation and tranquillity and forming a sort of cusp between the decades, a watershed from which one could look back upon the relatively small and simple California of vines and orchards, passenger trains and ferryboats, and forward to the teeming industrial commonwealth of today, incredibly transformed by population and technology.

All through my early years, the promise of the Exposition hovered in our minds. In that sense, Treasure Island affected everyone who lived in the Bay Area. It gave a slight elation to our lives. At the same time, our anticipations affected the Exposition, stamping it with the taste and prejudices of the 1930s: it was the end product, as well as the end, of those peculiar years.

My family lived in those days on a hillside street in Oakland — stucco houses, beds of marigolds and mirror plants clipped into green balloons. The street was so narrow that drivers had to park with the right wheels of their cars on the sidewalk. (My parents liked this parking problem. It discouraged traffic. Unfortunately, it also ruined a great Flexy hill.)

My days began with a nutritional ritual that was supposed to prevent colds: one large tablespoon of Upjohn's Codliver Oil, followed by a small glass of pulpy orange juice (very small, very pulpy) that my mother squeezed out by hand with a reamer. Afterward, a bowl of Hornby's Oats, a cup of Ovaltine, and off to school in corduroy knickers and a plaid wool windbreaker. Halfway up the hill there was a peppertree that arched across the pavement, forming a pungent tunnel, and, farther along, a hedge of pyracantha berries that you could strip off by the fistful and throw at the stop sign at the corner.

My school had a red tile roof and honey-colored window shades, and it was known as an Earthquake Trap. Every week or so the bell would ring insistently and we would get under our desks and count one-black-cat, two-black-cats, three-black-cats, up to one hundred, at which time the earthquake was presumed over and arithmetic resumed.

Most of the boys I knew collected pasteboard disks from the mouths of milk bottles. At the peak of my infatuation I had two hundred bottle tops — Fenton's, Shuey's, People's, and rarities from Reno and Los Angeles. We risked all in a game of Keepers, but a janitor saw us sailing bottle tops against the wall of the latrine and turned us in for gambling.

On Fridays the girls brought Shirley Temple dolls and photographs of the Dionne quintuplets to Show-and-Tell Time. I was in love with a girl who wore an enormous hair ribbon that rode like an open flower above one ear. We went into her playhouse one afternoon and performed an appendectomy on my teddy bear. He recovered, but he never squeaked again.

Most of the fathers on our street worked in San Francisco. They took the B Train and the ferry every morning and came home in the twilight, gently slapping their legs with the rolled-up, peach-colored news section of the *Call-Bulletin* as they trudged up the hill, picking their way among the parked cars and the Flexies. The newspapers carried headlines about the New Deal and the NRA and advertisements for puff-sleeved wash dresses at $1.95 and leg of lamb at nineteen cents a pound.

It was not the best of times, the early 1930s, even on narrow hillside streets in funny California. My father, using the old-fashioned language, speaks of it as "the hard times." For my parents, for all of their generation, the Depression was a long ordeal of courage and ingenuity. One of my aunts — Anglo-French extraction — was supporting her family by making and selling enchiladas. One day the firm my father worked for gave every one his weekly check and closed its doors forever.

To me, the Great Depression was an abstract image. I saw it mostly in vignettes of other people's poverty. It never occurred to me that we were suffering any deprivation. I looked down in pity on the Hooverville of tin-can shacks and cardboard walls that smoldered below the levee on the western edge of Sacramento. An old woman in a tawdry tiger fur stared at me from the line outside the Community Chest kitchen in Oakland, and a poor, grimy hobo with a patch on one eye — like the horrible pirate, Pew, who passed the Black Spot to Billy Bones in *Treasure Island* — came to our back door one afternoon, begging for a handout, leaning over me, breathing and squinting helplessly, and scared me out of my wits.

That winter the federal government was doling out 50,000,000 pounds of sauerkraut to keep hungry families alive. Down in Los Angeles there were 600,000 Utopians, clamoring for an end to private ownership of production and the establishment of a cooperative commonwealth. Upton Sinclair, the novelist, ran for governor on a majestic plan of tax abatement and public works called EPIC — "End Poverty in California" — and got more than a million votes.

In the midst of such creative fantasy, who could doubt that San Francisco would decide to build two bridges, each one the largest in the world? In those days, everything and nothing was impossible. The American faith in projects never dimmed. It was, after all, the generation of the Merchandise Mart, the Empire State Building, the Hoover Dam, an era of great disappointment and great accomplishment.

9

10   *A flower seller at Kearny and Market Streets displayed narcissus and carnations on a spring morning in the twenties.*

THE BEST OF TIMES, THE WORST OF TIMES

They were restless, problematical, uncertain years, the nineteen thirties: a time of ferryboats and tear gas bombs, flower stalls and Salvation Army soup. There were Big Game parties at the Mark and bread lines on Franklin Street, bay shrimp at Solari's and idle freighters on the bay. Mayor Angelo Rossi wore a white carnation in his button hole; pickets carried clubs on the Embarcadero.

The hero of Edward Dahlberg's hobo novel Bottom Dogs, bumming his way to California in the late twenties, scented "something special" in the San Francisco air — a "briny keenness that keyed one up to a ridiculous enthusiastic pitch."

In the thirties the briny keenness stayed, but the ridiculous enthusiasm faded.

The Ferry Building beckoned midnight commuters.

A leisurely boat ride
set the tempo of the day

*For almost a century passenger ferries plied the inland
sea between the bedroom cities of the East Bay and the
business center in downtown San Francisco. Patronage
reached 100,000 trips a day a few years before
the bridges drove the ferries from the bay. The morning
trip was brisk — a purposive throb of engines, a nip
of salt air, a rush to the coffee shop. Rounding Yerba
Buena Island, passengers checked their watches by
the groaning foghorn on the whitewashed cliff, where
countless ships had gone aground on murky days.
Then, with whitecaps prancing along the starboard
rail, the boat would lunge across the last two miles
of water toward the finger piers of the Embarcadero.
There would be a clang of bells, a shuddering resistance
in the paddle wheel, a boiling rush of foam below
the bow. With a screech and a thud, the ferry would
bury its nose between the straining wooden pilings
of the slip. The metal gangplank would crash down,
and the morning horde would thunder through the
the echoing corridors of the Ferry Building toward the*

line of streetcars waiting at the foot of Market Street.

The homeward trip was softer, quieter: bronze sky, pink water and a trailing plume of gulls above the wake. In the main saloon, shoppers from Fruitvale would slip off their shoes and dig into the latest Delineator *to catch up on the world of Jean Harlow and Norma Shearer. On the upper deck, captains of industry would share the joys of Culbertson contract bridge, Acme Beer and vicarious adventures in the* National Geographic.

A persistent reader could finish Anna Karenina *in a season or two of ferryboat commutes; a diligent one could conquer* The Remembrance of Things Past. *But the largo rhythm of the ferryboats was coming to an end. Before the decade was over, the faster tempo of the automobile paced the bay.*

A no-nonsense soda jerk manned the snack bar on a Southern Pacific ferry.

In the morning — coffee and doughnuts. In the evening — Golden Glow Beer. In either case — price, 15 cents.

Commuters strolled up Market Street on a summer morning in 1934.

Iron Monsters of the Market Street Railway and Municipal Railway paused cheek-by-jowl at Market and Annie Streets.

Hard times in funny, sunny California

The Depression that paralyzed the East was late in reaching the Pacific Coast, but its effect was deep and lasting. Its symptoms were the same everywhere: unemployment, bread lines, work relief projects. Panhandlers and apple peddlers on the city streets were constant reminders of the inexplicable collapse of the world's richest industrial society.

To the agricultural economy of California, the Depression also brought a unique and acutely painful new phenomenon — rural unemployment. In the prodigious fields and orchards of the Sacramento and the San Joaquin, workers were starving.

"Champagne Fred" Bell, heir to a fortune of $1 million in 1926, sold apples on a San Francisco corner in 1931.

Migrant families from drought-stricken Arkansas and Oklahoma searched for work in California's Central Valley.

A work relief project at San Francisco's Crocker-Amazon Playground followed the WPA principle of stretching the job to fit the manpower.

A family of emigrants from the Dust Bowl, a Social Security line and a crowded relief office — familiar scenes of the thirties.

Swinging billies and hurling tear gas bombs, police broke up a throng of strikers.

ILA pickets dominated the docks until truckloads of National Guardsmen took control.

A tragedy on the Embarcadero

At the depth of the Depression, 15,000 West Coast longshoremen quit work in the first coast-wide maritime strike in American history. Aided by teamsters, sailors, firemen, cooks and stewards, the International Association of Longshoremen effectively sealed the waterfront of San Francisco, the leading port on the Pacific. Week after week the strike dragged on, until the employers' association decided to reopen the port with hired strikebreakers.

On July 3, 1934, five trucks flanked by police patrol cars crossed the ILA picket lines at Pier 38. Strikers surged forward with bricks and stones. Police struck back with clubs and tear gas. On Independence Day, the employers declared the port "open" — but on the fifth, "Bloody Thursday," police and pickets fought hundreds of skirmishes from Rincon Hill to Fisherman's Wharf. Just outside ILA headquarters on Steuart Street, police fired into a crowd, killing Howard Sperry, a longshoreman, and Nick Bordoise, a cook. That night, Governor Frank Merriam ordered the National Guard to take over the waterfront.

Calling for justice, stevedores marched along the Embarcadero in July, 1934 (above right). A young longshoreman, clubbed in a riot, nursed a bruised cheek (left).

Flowers, flags and chalked inscriptions marked the spot where two strikers died.

The mourning and the wrath

Four days after the "Bloody Thursday" riot, 10,000 men and women trudged up Market Street in bitter silence, following the flower-covered caskets of two men whom most of them had never known. The strike that had begun 61 days before with demands for "better conditions, a shorter day and a living wage" had climaxed in martyrdom, fury and despair.

One by one, Bay Area labor unions voted for a general strike. On Monday, July 16, streetcars stopped running in San Francisco. Trucks and taxis left the streets. Markets, laundries, bars and service stations closed. Terrified by rumors of incipient revolution, volunteers barricaded residential neighborhoods in the East Bay and mobs of vigilantes raided Communist meeting rooms, broke windows, smashed presses and beat suspected radicals.

Within four days the general strike had collapsed. The maritime unions went back to work at the end of the month. But the settlement was only a lull in a decade of economic strife. In 1930 the labor unions in California had been weak in numbers and spirit; by the end of the decade they had reached unprecedented size and power.

Thousands of strikers assembled on Steuart Street in a funeral cortege for the riot victims.

When teamsters walked out in sympathy, strikebreakers overturned produce trucks and passersby snatched free peaches.

*As the general strike began, customers stripped grocery shelves
and lined up for gasoline. Yellow cabs stood idle. Shops closed,
and truck convoys with police escort brought food to the city.*

*It seemed impossible that
towers so far apart could ever
be linked by metal strands.*

Since the end of the Great War, people in northern California had been talking more or less seriously about building a suspension bridge across the Golden Gate. Hundreds of professed experts said it could not be built (on engineering grounds), should not be built (on aesthetic grounds), and probably would not be built (on financial grounds). But the counties to the north of the straits joined the city in forming a bridge district, and the voters approved a bond issue of $35,000,000. At the beginning of 1933, in the deeps of the Depression, the work began.

The other great bridge, the one between San Francisco and Oakland, had been a subject of debate and prophesy and ridicule for half a century. Nearly everyone said it would be convenient to have, but no one wanted to pay for it. The money came at last in the form of a $75,000,000 loan underwritten by the federal government. It was one of the last and grandest gestures of the Hoover Administration. Construction began six months after the start of the Golden Gate Bridge.

I was quite oblivious, of course, to the financial and political struggles and the engineering crises that attended the creation of the two great bridges. My newspaper reading was limited to daily episodes in the life of Uncle Wiggly, known also as "The Rabbit Gentleman," and the comic strips in the *Oakland Tribune* — Jane Arden, Mr. and Mrs., Harold Teen, The Timid Soul, Dan Dunn, Napoleon and Uncle Elby, Little Orphan Annie and Buck Rogers. ("Killer Kane's cosmic repulsors failed to check the fall of the huge planetoid fragment, and it crashed with the shock of a million atomic bombs . . . ")

I understand that it actually was a period of lively literary effort and artistic experimentation. In Chicago they put on a performance of Gertrude Stein's opera *Four Saints in Three Acts*, in which somebody says, "Pigeons on the shorter longer yellow grass alas alas." Midway through the show a small, red-faced man strode out to the bar in the foyer and announced he was going out and buy himself a straitjacket.

I, too, had conventional tastes. Every Sunday morning I would plow through "Aunt Elsie's Magazine for All the Girls and Boys," which came folded up with the *Tribune* funnies. Aunt Elsie maintained stringent editorial standards. Nobody ever asked for a straitjacket after reading Aunt Elsie's. In every issue she warned potential contributors about the perils of innovation and stream-of-consciousness writing.

"Here's the way to write a story for Aunt Elsie's Magazine — And the ONLY way," Aunt Elsie used to tell us, over and over. "Make it snappy — full of thrills. Make it ORIGINAL — all your own. NEVER COPY."

Being an unsnappy kid who went out of his way to avoid thrills, I never dared submit any of my copy to Aunt Elsie, but I have always tried to follow her editorial advice, especially that part about plagiarism.

In my innocence, my ignorance of engineering, politics, finance and avant-garde prose, I naturally regarded the two great bridges as objects of uncritical admiration. Like thousands of other California children, I kept a scrapbook of newspaper articles about the Bay Bridge, pasting the clippings down with a gummy mixture of flour, cornstarch and water, which wrinkled and stiffened the pages and rendered the collection repulsive to behold and quite useless as a historical document.

Riveters in hard hats fastened steel I beams across the sky.

From the deck of a ferry the central pillar looked like a windowless concrete skyscraper.

Cross-cut sample of main cable outside Ferry Building gave Bay Area children a tantalizing preview of the immense Bay Bridge.

Crossing the bay on the Key Route ferry, en route to see the Christmas windows at The White House and lunch on stuffed cabbage at the Russian Tea Room, we would crowd the upper deck to look at the huge caissons that had been floated into the bay and sunk, foot by foot, like a skyscraper growing downward, to form the foundations of the bridge. The shadows of the towers slithered along the promenade deck, casting a chill on the passengers at the rail. Looking up, we could see men in padded jackets clinging to brace beams in the sky.

According to the *Tribune*, the opening of the Bay Bridge was the greatest civic event in the Bay Area since the end of the World War. There were fireworks and school holidays, radio broadcasts, football games, chain-cuttings, ribbon-snippings and day-and-night parades. The newspaper coverage was prodigious. For weeks the Sunday rotogravure sections carried sepia pictures of the bridge, viewed from dangerous heights and reckless angles.

Although I do not remember the date when we first crossed the bridge, I am sure it was not the opening day. My father detested ceremonials and crowds. As soon as we had mastered our claustrophobia, however, we fulfilled our civic obligation to drive across and be properly astonished by the immensity of the roadway, the height of the towers and the caliber of the traffic tunnel through the center of Yerba Buena Island. What really impressed me most was the highway interchange east of the toll gate, the strands of concrete ribbon hurled into the sky, the cars weaving over and under like maypole dancers, and the eerie greenish luster of the sodium vapor lamps, turning carloads of blacks into whites and whites into parchment-colored corpses.

During the construction of the Bridge, I had developed a proprietary interest in the project. It was "Our Bridge," whereas the Golden Gate Bridge, which I later came to know and love much better than the San

Francisco-Oakland Bridge, seemed distant and almost sinister. I remember passing close to it only once, on the automobile ferry to Sausalito, yet I was haunted by the terror of that extraordinary venture, the swirling tides, the sudden fogs, the shrieking winds, the men who fell from that tremendous height and died. If the Golden Gate Bridge had depended on the courage of acrophobes like me, it would never have been built. I have always looked on it with awe — a sublime work of man, never to be superceded or discredited by the elaboration of a larger, more complex technology.

To most San Franciscans, the Golden Gate Bridge always was the more wonderful of the two, if only because it did not lead to Oakland. It encountered more financial and political resistance, required more imagination, excited more skepticism, took more time, claimed more lives — in short, demanded more courage, resourcefulness and energy from the people of California — than did the easier, longer, more expensive span across the bay. When the Golden Gate Bridge was opened at last, in May, 1937, a tremendous euphoria bubbled through the city.

Mayor Angelo Rossi's chauffeur was so enraptured by the spirit of fiesta that he bowled over a pedestrian in a crosswalk on the way to the fireworks. The Mayor's bodyguards whisked the victim up to City Hall, examined him for cuts and bruises, dosed him with Scotch whisky, settled him in the Mayor's reviewing stand and sent him on his way at dawn with a pasteboard key to the city and a scarcely noticeable limp.

TWO CAUSES FOR CELEBRATION

Nothing was more typical of the desperate bravado of the 1930s than the decision to construct the two largest bridges in the world over the troubled waters of San Francisco Bay. The San Francisco-Oakland Bay Bridge, more than eight miles long, took three years to build, employed an average of 6,500 men and cost $77,200,000. The Golden Gate Bridge, with a 4,200-foot center span, cost a mere $35,000,000 but took a year longer.

Not everyone thought the bridges were worth the effort. Katharine Fullerton Gerould, a writer of popular fiction and travel articles, was horrified: "When you have one of the most romantic approaches in all geography, why spoil it? Let the landowners of lovely Marin County stew in their own juice. Make the Sausalito ferry a 'floating palace;' beguile the half-hour journey with every vulgar pleasure; subsidize the commuters, if necessary; but in the interest of your own uniqueness, dear San Francisco, do not bridge the Golden Gate."

From the north tower of the half-finished Golden Gate Bridge, workmen had an incomparable view of San Francisco's modest profile.

Engineers and county officials wore hard hats and dark blue suits at a topping-off ceremony on the Marin tower.

Emperor Norton's ultimatum

San Francisco's mad monarch, Joshua Norton, Emperor of the United States and Protector of Mexico, decreed the bridging of the bay in 1869. The job finally was engineered half a century later by a commoner named Charles H. Purcell.

Purcell designed immense, watertight caissons of steel and timber, built and launched like ships at Moore Dry Docks in Oakland. Towed across the bay and anchored in position, each caisson became the base of a tower. As side walls grew higher, the box sank deeper, until it resembled a huge dry well, resting on bed rock. Filled with reinforced concrete, it became a firm foundation pillar. From then on, bridging the bay was a matter of building towers and spinning cables. Emperor Norton had always said it could be done, but other, saner San Franciscans were pleasantly surprised.

Two nights before the bridge opened, a motorist enjoyed the spooky, never-to-be-repeated thrill of crossing all alone.

Between Yerba Buena Island and San Francisco, engineers built two suspension spans, anchored at center to a caisson as tall as a 48-story building sunk in the bay.

Miss San Francisco, Miss Oakland and an International Queen showed up for the chain-cutting, while other Bay Area ladies (right) struck triumphant poses at mid-span on Opening Day, November 12, 1936.

The impossible span

Almost everyone knew the Golden Gate could not be bridged; but in this, as in other cases, almost everyone was wrong. To pin the structure to the cliffs, engineers had to bury four concrete anchor blocks that weighed 64,000 tons each. To establish a firm base for the south tower, they had to set up a concrete breakwater surrounding a lagoon as large as a football field, 1,100 feet off shore and swept by tides and storms. Three times, the trestle between this fender and the shore was demolished — twice by storms, once by a passing freighter. When divers began blasting a footing sixty-five feet under water, their dynamite shattered the bed rock. While geologists and seismologists publicly argued about the safety of the bridge, contractors dug thirty-five feet deeper and poured the base.

Even after towers were built and miles of cable spun, disaster haunted the bridge. Ten men fell to

Catwalks from tower to tower were braced with crossbars to reduce swaying.
Overhead wires carrried Roebling wheels that spun the main cables (above left).
A traveling derrick on wide, double rails carried steel girders for the traffic deck.

their deaths when a painting scaffold collapsed, tearing away the safety net.

In the public eye, Chief Engineer Joseph Strauss was the personification of the bridge, target of blame and glory. Engineering details were the work of his chief assistant, Clifford Paine, and resident engineer, Russell Cone; but it was Strauss, the poet and dreamer, the builder of great bridges in Russia, China, Egypt and Japan, who captured the imagination of the the world.

Victorious at last, Strauss wrote a poem to celebrate his greatest work. The rhyme is no match for Hart Crane's poem to the Brooklyn Bridge — but, then, Crane did not also build the Brooklyn Bridge.

At last the mighty task is done;
Resplendent in the western sun,
The bridge looms mountain high;
Its Titan piers grip ocean floor,
Its great steel arms link shore with shore,
Its towers pierce the sky . . .

The traffic deck of the bridge, suspended from hundreds of steel strands, grew outward from the towers to connect at mid-span.

A day of rejoicing

There was a nippy wind from the Pacific that morning in May, 1937, and pale strands of fog were whipping through the straits. Five thousand people waited at the barricades at dawn. A few had come on horseback, roller skates or bicycles, hoping to be the first to cross on any sort of vehicle, and one man was strutting back and forth on stilts. Many had come directly from an all-night bull at the Civic Auditorium, where George Jessel told jokes and Al Jolson sang. When the toll gates opened at 6:00, the crowd rushed forward with a shout of joy. A seventeen-year-old high school girl named Phyllis Kirschbaum was first in line. She was dressed in Mexican riding breeches and a black sombrero, as though she had anticipated making history. Behind her came sprinters in sweatsuits, skaters in slacks, chorus girls in penguin costumes. A man named Milton Pilhasky was pushing a pill box with his nose.

Fifteen thousand squeezed through the turnstiles every hour. The automatic counters gave up at 100,000, but the crowd kept coming. Bridge employees scooped up shovelsful of nickels and toted them to the counting house in buckets.

In the manner of conquistadores taking possession of a new territory, boys scratched their names on freshly painted girders and dug their initials into the asphalt roadbed. Families spread picnics in the center of the span. Parents took pictures of their children grinning possessively under 746-foot towers. Paper plates and tasseled hats soared in the wind and sailed into the bay. Ambulances trundled to and fro, dispensing bandages and ankle tape. Shortly after noon, a bank of fog slithered under the bridge, oozed up like steam and blotted out the towers. By nightfall, 200,000 votaries had trod the span of gold.

For a few months after the bridge was finished, ferryboats continued to cross the bay. To sentimental San Franciscans, it was like living in two worlds.

A prescient or pessimistic person might have sensed, even then, that the world was turning away from parades and carnivals; but civic boosters are seldom prescient and never pessimistic. We enjoyed another week of holidays and marching bands. There were sheaths of redwood bark around the lamps on lower Market Street and live sheep browsing on Polk Street. Press agents from Hollywood and Detroit sneaked an actor (Wayne Morris) and a car (DeSoto) across the bridge to score two firsts for the *Guinness Book of World Records*.

That the celebration also should include a world's fair was the inspiration of a real estate man named Joseph Dixon, who proposed the idea in a letter to the *San Francisco News* in 1933. The *News* responded with a few words of editorial approval, suggesting that Dixon ought to get the first season pass for his originality. The idea must have occurred to others almost simultaneously, however, for it swept through the city councils and business promotion bureaus of northern California like news of a tax repeal. Soon the councils were bombarding one another with resolutions saying "Best of Luck" and "Congratulations on your new venture" and "We're behind you" and that kind of thing.

A group of sponsors in San Francisco, based informally at the Chamber of Commerce, spent several months picking a location and raising funds. First, they hired two San Francisco architects to study seven or eight places that someone thought might be suitable for an exposition. This procedure, known in administrative quarters as "loving the subject to death," usually results in the quiet strangulation of embryonic projects, but in this case the architects took their assignment seriously. They examined and rejected Golden Gate Park because it was "too fragile," China Basin because it was too ugly, Candlestick Point because it was too squalid, and Lake Merced because it was too far from the center of things (besides being notoriously foggy all summer). The only appealing spot, apparently, was a 735-acre reef lying under the surface of the bay just north of Yerba Buena Island. Test borings taken from a barge showed that the reef could support a man-made island.

By no coincidence the Yerba Buena Shoals also had been singled out several years earlier by the San Francisco Junior Chamber of Commerce as an ideal location for an airport. (Junior chambers of commerce all over the country were obsessed with airports.) Henry Eickoff, Jr., the J.C.'s aviation chairman, got out a press release praising the exposition site committee for its clarity of vision and pointing out that the island, after doing service as an exposition, could become a permanent airport. Whichever one made money could pay for the one that didn't.

A few days after the architects published their report, Mayor Rossi's exposition committee turned itself into a public corporation to raise funds. The president was Leland W. Cutler, an insurance man, who also was an officer of the Chamber of Commerce, a trustee of Stanford University, a prominent Republican and a member of virtually every civic betterment organization in the city; and the other members were merchants, bankers, real estate men, lawyers, accountants and other recognizable figures of the downtown landscape. Almost immediately, they sent Cutler to Washington, D.C., to plead for money.

Several members of the San Francisco Board of Supervisors wanted the fair on the "mainland" of the city — "a five-cent streetcar ride from any place in San Francisco," one of them said. Their opposition culminated in a characteristic supervisorial debate that lasted from two o'clock one afternoon until three o'clock the next morning. At one point, Supervisor James McSheehy, who is still remembered for his original contributions to American idiom, cried out in exasperation: "Everybody loves Le Cutler, and we all love him, but he don't know the rump of the common people like I do!"

In conclusion the Board decided to appraise the people's rump by putting the key question to a public vote. It turned out that the people were in favor of building an island but were against issuing municipal bonds to pay for it.

Luckily, Cutler brought word from Washington that Harry Hopkins, head of the federal government's Works Progress Administration (the now-legendary WPA) had agreed to grant San Francisco $3,800,000 to build an airport if the exposition company could raise $760,800 locally to contribute to the project. The local committee hooted when Cutler told them he had a verbal promise to that effect from both Hopkins and President Franklin D. Roosevelt. No right-thinking Republican businessman believed those two on oath. After much head-shaking and eye-rolling, the sponsors agreed to scrape up their share. The government, in the end, contributed more than twice as much as Roosevelt and Hopkins had promised.

When all the financing, contracting and administration had been fitted together, the island was one of the most complicated joint ventures anyone in California had ever seen. It involved not only the WPA (which put up most of the money), but also the War Department (which contracted through the Army Corps of Engineers to build the island), the Public Utilities Commission of San Francisco (which expected to run the future airport), the Public Works Administration (which paid for the administration building and two permanent aircraft hangars), the exposition corporation and the Navy. The Army Engineers hoped also to involve half a dozen local dredging companies, but the dredgers sensed trouble and declined to bid for the job. The Engineers finally took it on themselves, using government equipment and dredges rented from various private owners. Risk capital was a wary bird in those days, as it had cause to be.

In its way, the island was a marvel of engineering — not a masterpiece to outclass the Golden Gate Bridge, of course, nor even the Bay Bridge, but unquestionably clever. The Chamber of Commerce and other palm-bearers spread word that the 400-acre land fill would be the largest man-made island on earth, a claim that probably could have been disputed by the engineers of some of the large polders in the Netherlands. The Dutch, from politeness or preoccupation, never pressed the point.

The Army Engineers started work in March, 1936, months before the bridges were finished, and put the last touches on the island a year and a half later, right on schedule. First, they barged 287,000 tons of boulders out to Yerba Buena Shoals and built a sort of seawall surrounding a rectangular lagoon a mile long and two-thirds of a mile wide. Then, working northward from the shallow end, they began filling the lagoon with sand and mud pumped up from the bottom of the bay. The technique resembled the way a reef of coral builds an atoll, although hardly anyone in the Bay Area knew much about coral atolls in those days. The idea came from W.P. Day, who was the architect associated with George W. Kelham in finding the site for the exposition, and the army officer in command of the project was Frederic B. Butler. Years later, General Butler was general manager of the San Francisco International Airport and Day was the chief architect of the airport terminal buildings, but the airport was miles from Treasure Island.

The dredges worked twenty-four hours a day, sucking up millions of cubic yards of sand, peat, fossilized ferns, snails, fish, shellfish and the bones and tusks of extinct animals. Thousands of seagulls, swirling around like flakes of snow, came to feast on the seafood. When ferries from Berkeley churned past, a few opportunistic birds would peel off and soar in the wake, screaming for sandwich crusts and morsels of breakfast pastries, but most of the gulls gave up the old trans-bay commute in favor of the fat life in the new suburb. They were still around, cadging popcorn, when the fair began.

Even before the outlines of the island had taken shape, the engineers built a causeway of earth and gravel, sloping down from Yerba Buena Island, to connect the exposition site to the Bay Bridge. One morning in August a few thousand consular representatives, Boy Scouts, photographers and city fathers trudged down the road to take formal possession of the tideflat, which was still damp and gooey.

Mayor Rossi hailed "the newest of our insolent possessions," and Governor Frank Merriam sank a gold-plated spade into the muck. A business representative from the counties north of the bay brought along a redwood chest filled with newspapers and other ephemera and buried it at the site of the administration building. The massed flags of France and England, Italy, Japan and Nazi Germany whipped in the wind.

I was not there, of course. I had just turned nine, and I had no consular connections. But the ceremony was pictured and described in the newspapers the next day, shoulder-to-shoulder with a report from Spain, where four insurgent columns were closing on the capital. At that time, no one had heard of the "fifth column" inside Madrid.

Treasure Island was a few square yards of gooshy mud in spring, 1936, when Exposition President Leland Cutler (right) rowed out from Yerba Buena Island with George Smith (left) and Kent Dyson to plant a flag designating it "Site of the 1939 World's Fair." Cutler, a resourceful man, wore rubber overshoes.

In August, 1936, they broke ground, so to speak, for the Exposition. The mushy soil and murky weather made the ceremony seem premature, but a full complement of dedicators showed up. Governor Frank Merriam handled the shovel. Boy Scouts from Old St. Mary's Church in Chinatown trooped the colors, and Leland Cutler (with shovel) and M.O. Goldman (with box) planted a redwood chest filled with plans for the fair. The parking lot of the Administration Building now covers this Time Capsule, seriously impairing its usefulness as a historical resource.

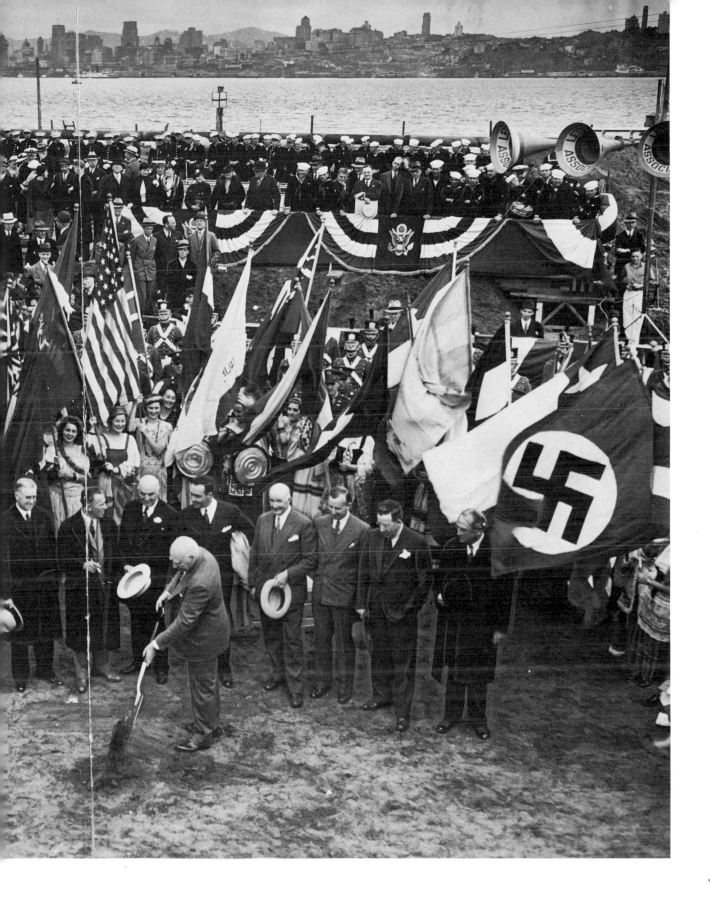

I was inspired that summer to acquire an insolent possession of my own. Skip Johnson and I built a skull-shaped body of land, more or less completely surrounded by water, on the shoals of Trestle Glen Creek. We adopted the W.P. Day-Frederic Butler engineering principles — first, a cofferdam of rocks, then a backfill with sand and gravel, working upstream; but we took considerably less time about it than the Army Engineers, and we did considerably less boasting.

Like its model, our island was going to offer a variety of wholesome family entertainments. There were twilight illuminations of benzene in a Trupak tomato can, downstream wading parties, tadpole hunting and skyrides on a rope knotted over the limb of a bay tree. On festive afternoons we lighted a red drip candle atop the theme building, a cairn of rocks at the jawbone end of the island.

Trestle Glen Creek, unfortunately, was the *cloaca maxima* of the neighborhood. Green slime flowed past the exposition. Gases drifted around. The miasma finally drove us away, although we did cook supper one evening and discussed an overnight encampment that never came off.

Winter rains dissolved the island, and time has swept its name and its precise location from my mind. I dredge up this fossil tooth of recollection merely to show how island-building affected our thoughts. It was not that we lacked other forms of entertainment — after all, those were the rollicking days of ice cream price wars and one-man flights to Hawaii, dog races in El Cerrito and overnight passenger steamers to Los Angeles. But the new island, the great man-made island in the bay, offered the prospect of commercial recreation compared to which our usual amusements had a frontier simplicity.

My family, for one, seldom paid to be entertained. On weekends, we usually would "take a drive" over the Fish Ranch Road and through the orchards to Walnut Creek, a village at the foot of Mount Diablo, where there was a drugstore famous for ice cream sodas. On Sunday evening, exhausted by all this excitement, we listened to Eddie Cantor with Rubinoff and His Violin. The radio was bell-shaped — Spanish Mission style, I suppose. It had wooden grille work and metallic brocade, and the call letters of all the important local stations were printed on the tuning dial — KROW, KPO, KLX and so on.

Our appliances, I must admit, were shocking. Cars had running boards and radiator ornaments. Washing machines were equipped with rubber wringers. Refrigerators stood on legs and had cylindrical white ventilators on top. At my house we had, instead, an icebox made of varnished golden oak. The Union Ice Company sent a truck through the neighborhood twice a week, and a muscular man in a black rubber apron brought in a fifty-pound block of ice and lifted it into the top compartment with a pair of tongs. As the ice melted it dripped down into a cake pan on the floor. This pan usually overflowed at night because my mother forgot to empty it before going to bed. In a last stand against mechanization my father drilled a hole in the floor and put in a funnel and hose to drain off the nightly thaw. A month or two after that improvement, we had our first refrigerator.

Small wonder that the promise of visiting an island crowded with art museums, theaters and Ferris wheels inflamed our dreams. We watched it growing in the harbor, beyond the pillars of the bridge, third member of a brilliant trinity of technological miracles. Eugen Neuhaus, the distinguished art historian and critic at the University of California, was tremendously steamed up about the island. He saw it as an opportunity to create a whole new city, totally devoted to culture and entertainment, free of all the architectural blemishes of ordinary urban real estate. This island, like the island of San Giorgio, opposite the piazza of St. Mark in Venice, would seem to float in the midst of a vast lagoon, visible from all the cities on the shore, yet far-off and romantic, swept about by limpid water.

That an exposition in such surroundings would be beautiful was almost inevitable. That it would also be conservative, eclectic and sentimental was inevitable, too, given the team of architects chosen to design the buildings and lay out the grounds. At the head of the group was George Kelham, who had been chief architect for the 1915 Panama-Pacific International Exposition, a neoclassical tour de force that held strong, nostalgic power over a whole generation of Californians. When Kelham died in 1937, the architectural command passed to Arthur Brown, Jr., another veteran of the Panama-Pacific and designer of the San Francisco City Hall, a jewel of simulated baroque style. Like many San Franciscans of their age, Kelham and Brown were willing to risk being called old-fashioned and derivative so long as they were not called radical.

The men around them were a marvel of harmonious collaboration, products of the Paris Beaux-Arts, artistic conservatives, Bohemian Clubbers — the old guard of San Francisco's large architectural establishment: Lewis P. Hobart, William Gladstone Merchant, Timothy L. Pflueger, Ernest E. Weihe. During a period when architectural jobs were scarce

Treasure Island International Airport inspired federal spending and artist's drawings but never went into operation.

41

and there were no urban renewal projects, public housing contracts or regional shopping centers to keep the wolf from the drafting-room door, all of them had survived and even prospered by clinging to a genteel, pseudo-European tradition of surface decoration. If any of them had heard of the Berlin Bauhaus, Mies van der Rohe, Frank Lloyd Wright or Le Corbusier, he had seldom allowed that influence to show in his work.

With characteristic faith in nineteenth century values, the architects decreed that the fairgrounds should resemble a grandiose imperial city — exactly the sort of idealized city that might have been dreamed up half a century earlier by D.H. Burnham or Frederick Law Olmsted. Three permanent buildings (an airport terminal and two aircraft hangars) would occupy the south end of the island. The terminal would serve as an administration building for the fair, the hangars as an art gallery and a hall of aviation. The rest of the exhibit halls would be large, rectangular sheds, grouped to enclose vast malls and courtyards and decorated on the outside to look like palaces. There would be no modernist nonsense about form following function or less being more.

As for the method of construction, that too would follow the traditions established in 1915. The pavilions would be framed with wood, covered with laths and then sheathed in burlap and stucco. There would be no hint here of the technological developments that would revolutionize American architecture within a few years — no modules of pre-cast, pre-stressed concrete, no raw steel beams, no molded plywood, no plastic tents, structural aluminum or glass curtain walls. New York had preempted the future by naming its fair "The World of Tomorrow." San Francisco took a firm grip on the past. Virtually the only innovation accepted by the board of architects was a decorative process called Zonolite, which involved spraying the wet stucco surfaces with heated flakes of mica in nineteen official tints, from Evening Star Blue to Pebble Beach Coral.

The layout of the grounds was dictated by the lusty west wind that blows through the Golden Gate almost every day of the year. To shelter the courtyards, the architects planned a bulwark of buildings, eighty feet high, stretching for a quarter of a mile along the west side of the island. Ernest Weihe spent hours with cardboard baffles, electric fans and chicken feathers, trying to figure out how to get customers through the barricade while keeping the wind out. His solution was to build immense vertical baffles, like the fly wings of a stage, at several points along the west wall. Visitors could dart through these louvers, watery-eyed and

Barges, trucks and tugboats brought 4,000 trees to Treasure Island. Lifted from California gardens, they weighed up to forty tons each.

tousled, and find shelter on the leeward side. Unfortunately, large areas of the island, including the amusement zone and the parking lot, were on the weather side. People were always spreading rumors about Pekinese puppies and small children being wafted off toward Albany by the afternoon gales.

Whenever the architects were asked to explain the cultural and historic roots of the Exposition Style, they would avow that the eighty-foot bulwark had been inspired by the walled cities of Cambodia; but I suspect that this inspiration occurred *after* the committee had decided to adopt a decorative motif they called "Pacific Basin," allegedly borrowed from Mayan, Incan, Malayan and Cambodian archeology.

The reasons for choosing a Pacific theme were obvious. San Francisco always has fancied itself to be the "Gateway of the Pacific," at least for those who are looking toward the Pacific from the northeastern shore; and the decor was an inducement to nations bordering the Pacific to send exhibits.

The reasons for selecting Central American and Indochinese art as the primary sources were not so clear. Why not Eskimo, Maori or Japanese? No one ever explained.

At the same time, the architects were conscious of the Venetian analogy noticed by Professor Neuhaus. Their final plans called for a slender central tower, rising 400 feet above the pale blue lagoon and the pale Zonolite buildings. It looked for all the world like a Venetian campanile, or maybe a Tuscan campanile. At any rate, it was not a Cambodian campanile.

These comments about architecture, I admit, are afterthoughts. When the fair was in construction, few San Franciscans were either critical or conscious of its architectural style. To the contrary, nearly everyone was entranced by the prospect of seeing with his own eyes immense Cambodian elephant towers, glistening with Santa Clara Apricot and Polynesian Brown Zonolite, and was dazzled by the designers' brilliant idea of using the same motif to decorate the hoods of Elephant Trains to carry footsore visitors around the island.

The island that Skip Johnson and I built in Trestle Glen Creek never reached the stage of architectural embellishment. A woman who lived nearby warned us we were trespassing, and we were afraid the sight of a Pacific Basin tower of scrap lumber rising from the creekbed would provoke her to call the police. Nor did we attempt any landscaping, although the newspapers printed challenging reports about the technical problems of raising a garden on the Yerba Buena Shoals.

To begin with, the mud dredged from the bottom of the bay was too salty to support anything but marsh grass. After the surface had dried off, the Army Engineers drilled 300 holes, twenty-five feet deep, and pumped out millions of gallons of brine. Heavy winter rains (the same rains, I suppose, that made our island one with Nineveh and Tyre) leached out most of the remaining salt. Then, gardeners laid on tons of gypsum and barge-loads of rich loam from the Sacramento River delta. Finally, during the summer before the fair began, they brought in thousands of full-grown trees and hundreds of thousands of shrubs, vines, bulbs and bedding plants.

Most of the small plants grew at a Park Department nursery in San Francisco, but the large trees came from gardens and orchards around the Bay Area. An entire olive grove, transplanted from Napa County, lined one of the major avenues. The Alameda-Contra Costa County building had a lawn of nine-year-old sod lifted in chunks from a garden in Piedmont, and the outdoor theater of the Federal Building nestled in a forest of tall pines and redwoods, uprooted from the preserves of the Department of Agriculture.

One of my mother's friends decided to donate a magnolia that had outgrown its place on a quiet street in Oakland. A crew of men came by in a truck, tore up several square yards of paving around the tree and built a six-foot box around the roots. Next morning they lifted out the whole thing with a crane and trundled it away.

My mother's friend was proud of her contribution to the fair, although her front garden looked strangely empty. When the Exposition opened, however, she felt a longing to see her tree again. She searched the island in growing confusion. Not one but dozens of magnolias resembled her tree. At last she found a magnolia that conformed in every respect to the one she remembered. Her eyes filled with tears, and she sat down on a bench, clutching her guidebook, and stared at her tree for ten minutes. It was surrounded by drifts of white narcissus and yellow tulips and pink clouds of cherry blossoms. It made her think of a lost soul, lifted into paradise.

After that, my mother's friend stopped by to see her tree each time she went to the fair. Sometimes it was floating in a froth of white begonias, sometimes in a fragrant pink sea of asters or chrysanthemums. She often took friends to see it, as to a public levee, and they would sit there on the bench, resting their feet and eating sandwiches and looking at the tree, feeling a strange, almost fraternal affinity with the Exposition and its plant life.

Not many visitors had such an intimate relationship with any of the island's 4,000 trees, but everyone who saw the gardens of the Exposition felt they had been planted for his personal delight. They were the creation, mainly, of Julius L. Girod, a San Francisco park superintendent and protégé of John McLaren, the chief druid of Golden Gate Park. Girod had a magnificent budget of $1,800,000 from the Works Progress Administration to nurse, transport and install vegetation on the salty waste. He used the money, as the WPA intended him to do, on the most labor-squandering of all garden arrangements — acres and acres of seasonal bulbs and annual flowers, all planted, pinched back, fertilized and cultivated by hand. Out of 6,000 workers on the island during the last few months before the Exposition opened, more than 1,200 were Girod's employees. It was said that Harry Hopkins, back in Washington, was in rapture over the size of the payroll.

The masterpiece of Girod's Bureau of Horticulture was a ground planting of more than a million succulent ice plants covering twenty-five acres on the exposed west side of the island. This enormous carpet of mesembryanthemums — orange, red, yellow, pink, mauve and magenta — was indifferent to salt spray and ocean wind. It glowed cheerfully on mad March days when the fronds of the Washington palms were lashing overhead like swordsmen in mortal combat. An inventive publicist named it the Persian Prayer Rug; but this geographic extension of the Pacific Basin never took hold. Most people, recognizing that ice plant lawns were clearly indigenous to California, simply called it "The Magic Carpet," and slipped choice cuttings into their coat pockets.

Many of the species in the Carpet were natives of the California beaches; others, originally imported from South Africa, had been thriving for generations in rock gardens and patios around the Bay Area. Eric Walther, a San Francisco horticulturist who had been introduced to the study of succulents by the distinguished botanist Alice Eastwood, gathered the parent plants from collectors in San Diego, Berkeley and other coastal cities and propagated them at the Arboretum in Golden Gate Park. Of all the architectural and floral features of the Exposition, the Magic Carpet set the most enduring style. Its mark is on front yards and freeway embankments all over California.

After a rest period at San Francisco's Balboa Park, mature trees up to seventy feet in height reached Treasure Island. The landscaping plan also called for 800,000 annuals, 400,000 perennials, 250,000 tulips.

THE BIRTH OF A MARINE VENUS

Treasure Island was San Francisco's third great project of the thirties, a little sister of the bridges.

Like most large undertakings in that stagnant decade, the project depended on government aid — $3.8 million from the New Deal's Works Progress Administration. To seal the contract, business sponsors in San Francisco scraped together $760,780 in matching funds, a down-payment on a world exposition that would occupy the man-made island for a year or two. When the fair was over, two hangars and an administration building would remain. The 400-acre pancake of bay mud would be criss-crossed with 4,000-foot runways (the ultimate in airport demand in those days) and the Bay Area would have a magnificent central terminal, forever free of obstruction to the north, east or west.

On February 11, 1936, the Army Corps of Engineers began piling mud and sand in the shallows north of Yerba Buena Island. In places the shoal lay only two feet below the surface, and the new island began to rise from the water within a few days. One dredge sucked material from the bottom of the lagoon (the future "Port of Trade Winds") between Yerba Buena and the fill area, while other dredges carried sand from "borrow areas" in the west bay — Presidio Shoals, Alcatraz Shoals and Knox Shoals. Barges brought 287,000 tons of boulders to construct a three-mile rim around the fill.

Ultimately, the Engineers employed eleven dredges: stately pipeline dredges that fed sand directly onto the new island through long tubes; hopper dredges that pumped mud into huge bins and wafted it slowly across the bay; and towering clamshell dredges that scooped up tons of muck in their jaws and deposited it in waiting barges.

For eighteen months the dredges worked night and day. They raised 25,000,000 cubic yards of fill, including the fangs of extinct animals, fossilized ferns, peat moss, shrimps, crabs, snails and small fry. To leach the salt out, the Engineers drilled 300 wells in the surface of the island and pumped millions of gallons of brine back into the bay.

Precisely on schedule, the fill was finished. The dredges went off duty on August 24, 1937. But, in a geographical sense, the island was still in the making. Its northern end, laid on a base of spongy mud, was expected to sink a foot a year for the next seven years. No buildings could be constructed there. Wind-swept and unreliable, the north end served as a 12,000-car parking lot for the Exposition.

The Triumphal Arch, though temporary, rested on 75-foot pilings. The 400-foot Tower of the Sun, framed with light steel girders, required 200 pilings sunk 90 feet into the squashy island soil.

Great staircases and wind baffles forming the west wall of the Exposition looked as substantial as Angkor Wat, but they actually were Douglas fir planks coated with tinted stucco.

50 *South Tower, flanking the Court of the Moon, was stuccoed in "Evening Star Blue." Among other colors in the Exposition's official palette were Santa Barbara Taupe, Death Valley Mauve and Santa Clara Apricot.*

Ettore Cadorin's "Evening Star" (here being bathed for her unveiling) was the public favorite, but O.C. Malmquist's gilded "Phoenix," a symbol of the resurrection of San Francisco after the 1906 earthquake and fire, was unquestionably the most prominent. Glistening with gold leaf, the 22-foot wrought iron ornament topped the Tower of the Sun. Newspapers frequently had to reassure readers that the head had not fallen off.

*A grader smoothing the surface of the Temple Compound
was one of dozens at work in the last weeks before the fair opened.
More than 6,000 workmen painted, planted and groomed the island.*

Between thinking up names for flower beds and adjectives for Pacific Basin architecture, the publicists had their work cut out for them. Their main problem was to convince several million families to come to California a few years hence to see an unspecified show on an unfinished island. The exhibitors were counting on twenty million paid admissions, and at least fifty percent of them would have to come from out-of-state.

Clyde Milner Vandeburg, a specialist in the rarified art of promoting world fairs, moved in. First off, he suggested calling the 400-acre pancake of bay mud "Treasure Island," a name that was supposed to sound relaxed and tropical and to conjure up visions of buried gold and nostalgic images of San Francisco in the days when Robert Louis Stevenson lived on Bush Street. Later, Vandeburg invited former President Herbert Hoover to appear in a prospector's hat and pan for gold at the ground-breaking of the Mines, Metals and Machinery Building. Mr. Hoover was delighted, although not surprised, to turn up a few flecks of gold.

ON SAN FRANCISCO BAY

1939 WORLD'S FAIR

GOLDEN GATE INTERNATIONAL EXPOSITION

"He reminded me that the name 'Treasure Island' was altogether fitting, because the soil we had pumped up from the bay to build the island was refuse washed down the Sacramento River from the gold dredges far inland," Vandeburg recalls. "He told me that if a man worked hard ten hours a day he could probably pan about a dollar's worth of gold on Treasure Island."

Vandeburg also made up a slogan to wow transportation companies and travel agencies: "See All the West in '39." Another creative aphorist decided that the whole affair should be entitled "A Pageant of the Pacific," although it was not going to be a pageant and had virtually nothing to do with the Pacific. The architects played along, gamely chattering nonsense about Chichen-Itza and Angkor Wat.

All in all, it was pretty vague, but the peculiar American talent for advertising thrives on lack of substance. The publicity office brought in mule teams, Boy Scout troops and dancers from the chorus line at the Bal Tabarin. James Earle Fraser's statue "The End of the Trail," a favorite of visitors to the 1915 Exposition, somehow wound up in the foreground of several promotional photographs, giving the impression that it, the American Indian, the Old West and *fin de siècle* statuary all would play major parts in the fair, which they did not do. No one seems to have resented this mild deception.

Premature souvenirs began to trickle out of the lofts of Mission Street and into the cocktail bars of America: napkins and matchbooks, ashtrays and highball glasses, embossed with decalcomanias of elephant towers

Fraser's "End of the Trail" somehow was mixed into the Pacific Basin and pirate themes.

and Washington palms, gossamer bridges and rectangular islands. Around the bay there was a sudden proliferation of Exposition markets, florists and seafood grottoes, a few of which are still in business.

The one-piece bathing suit emerged as an important facet of Pacific Basin style. Dozens of young women in one-piece bathing suits marched up stairways and under arches, gesturing grandly toward the distant battlements. The young women were never out and around when I visited the fair, probably because on most days they would have died of cold, but there is plenty of photographic evidence that they ranged freely over the island during the Late Construction period.

I mark this pioneering use of the one-piece bathing suit in architectural propaganda as one of the permanent legacies of Treasure Island. It came at a time when the Hollywood film industry was groping its way out of a long gothic twilight, peopled by such non-swimmers as Marie Dressler, the Marx Brothers and Wallace Berry, and it opened the way for the later success of Betty Grable, Esther Williams and Jane Russell, no small accomplishment.

Ultimately, Treasure Island hired a full-time "Theme Girl," a young ballet dancer named Zoe Dell Lantis. The "theme," in this case, turned out to be piracy, which was evidently consistent with islands and treasures, if not with Pacific Basin. Dressed in a Peter Pan sunsuit and seven-league boots, Zoe Dell peeked through spyglasses, cracked open treasure chests and struck piratish poses for the news cameras.

Before the fair opened, Zoe Dell made a cross-country trip in full regalia, stopping along the way to "publicize the Grand Canyon," as her advance agents put it. Most places, she got yards of newspaper space, although her three-cornered hat and Spanish cape failed to arouse much enthusiasm in Manhattan. Mayor LaGuardia refused to be photographed with a female pirate in shorts, and Zoe Dell had to wrap up in a fur coat. People in New York had their own fair to think about.

New York was officially displeased with our Exposition. When Grover Whelan, the president of the New York Fair, got wind of the competing show, he put in a long distance call to Leland Cutler and asked, "What does San Francisco mean by having an exposition the same year as New York?" Cutler bounced back: "The only answer I can think of, Mr. Whalen, is what does New York mean having an exposition the same year as San Francisco?" After that riposte, Whalen and Cutler never got along well, although Cutler admitted they had one thing in common: "The day of world's fairs was over before we started and neither of us knew it."

New Yorkers in the federal government tried to force San Francisco to postpone its Exposition; but President Roosevelt, hoping that competition would stimulate interest in both fairs, maintained the government's commitment to San Francisco. Eventually, Washington and New York both sent peaceable missions to Treasure Island. LaGuardia came out for dinner, and Eleanor Roosevelt performed a ceremonial groundbreaking on the site of the Federal Building.

"Her one condition," George Creel wrote in his memoirs, "was that she would not be asked to pull any levers or 'ride in anything,' and I gave her the promise with hand on my heart. What I did not count on was the owner of a big steam shovel and his pride in it. No sooner was Mrs. Roosevelt installed in the flower-garlanded seat than he plunged off hell-bent, plowing through puddles and plunging into ditches. I raced after him, ruining a perfectly good pair of striped trousers, but the proud gent had gone a full three hundred yards over rough terrain before I could bring him to a halt. Mrs. Roosevelt's famous smile was conspicuously absent as we helped her down . . . "

Several months after Mrs. Roosevelt's exciting ride, the President himself arrived on a naval cruiser. He toured the island by car and spoke at a luncheon in the administration building. The trip cost Mr. Roosevelt considerable effort, and the promoters of the Exposition looked on it as an endorsement of great consequence, as did all the local functionaries of the Democratic party who happened to be invited to lunch.

A BEAUTIFUL BARRAGE OF BALLYHOO

Two great traditions of American press agentry — the Give-Us-a-Little-Smile-Baby School and the Monumental Snow Job—came together in anticipation of the Golden Gate International Exposition. While Professor Eugen Neuhaus was tantalizing East Bay women's clubs with lectures on the art treasures of the Exposition, crass photographers imported "honey-haired Dorothy Drew, one of Sally Rand's Music Box lovelies" to the island to give a little smile.

"She was so intrigued with the Tower of the Sun that she prevailed upon Artist Leland Clifford to sketch the skyline on her back so she could take it with her," the press release said.

Nobody believed it, even in the deluded thirties, but what editor could resist that picture?

The Roosevelt magic

They turned on the fountains and draped bunting on unfinished buildings when President Roosevelt toured the island with Mayor Rossi (in the jump seat), Governor Merriam (center) and a cohort of body-guards. At lunch the President jawed with George Creel while Oakland's Mayor McCracken hovered overhead and Merriam clutched notes for his speech.

58

Eleanor Roosevelt made a separate visit to boost the fair. U.S. Commissioner George Creel, in top hat and tails, met the train and promised that Mrs. Roosevelt would not have to "ride in anything." She wound up at the wheel of a steam shovel, breaking ground for the Federal Building.

The President's Treasure Island lunch in July, 1938, left scars among local Democrats. "Only one thousand guests could be crowded into the room . . . and ten thousand Democrats demanded invitations," Creel recalled in his memoirs. "As the favored thousand sat down, the rage of those outside had the roar and beat of a tidal wave." Creel, a muckraking journalist and one-time candidate for governor of California, served as toastmaster, introduced Republican Governor Frank Merriam as "one of the few survivors of a once-great tribe." In later years, disillusioned with Roosevelt, maverick Creel switched tribes.

An act of piracy

Zoe Dell Lantis had good legs, a minor-league movie contract and an inexhaustible smile when Treasure Island hired her as "Theme Girl" early in 1938. Her perky pirate costume had nothing to do with the Pacific Basin, but the high-heeled boots and cut off pants hinted at raffish adventure. Carl Wallen's publicity shots of Zoe Dell sparkled with the careless charm Americans associate with San Francisco — and the sweet kid would do practically anything to get her picture in the papers.

Touring coast to coast, Zoe Dell posed with an Indian chief in Taos, drove a bulldozer, stood mock trial in Charleston, rode in a hansom cab and did nip-ups at the site of the New York World's Fair. She even consented to "publicize the Grand Canyon," as her advance men put it, by leaping over a crevasse seven feet wide and 900 feet deep.

"I wore high heels," Zoe Dell explained later, "because I didn't want my ankles to look thick."

Sterling Sherwin, a San Francisco songwriter, was inspired to immortalize the Theme Girl in song: "You're the one light, the sunlight / In my heart / You're my big thrill, Always will be until / The end of all time shall us part / Our hearts beat in time /And our souls seem in rhyme / You're like heavenly music from above / You reign supreme / And seem my theme / Of every dream and scheme / My dream girl, my Theme Girl of Love . . ."

From the official songbook of the Exposition, "Song of San Francisco."
Copyright 1967 by Harmony House, Mill Valley, Calif.

Some visiting engineers encountered the Give-Us-a-Little-Smile-Baby style of public relations.

I have to admit that President Roosevelt's visit made no particular impression on me. It was an adults-only event, like the conference in Munich that autumn between Neville Chamberlain and Adolf Hitler to straighten out the future of Europe. I was more interested in participatory affairs — school holidays, parades and special radio programs with Edna Fisher stomping out Treasure Island songs on the KPO organ. Above all, I liked fiestas. Everyone in California liked fiestas in the 1930s. They were thought to be indigenous to the West and good for retail trade. I date my private endorsement of the Exposition, my personal fever of anticipation, from the week of costume parties and excused time that immediately preceded the opening of the gates.

Like most California celebrations, Fiesta Week had an "Old West" decor, which added a new layer of symbolism to the Cambodian, pirate and one-piece bathing suit motifs. Mayor McCracken urged the women of Oakland to cast off their puff-shouldered swagger coats and bolero dresses and deck themselves in scarlet fandango skirts; Mayor Rossi of San Francisco put on a black sombrero trimmed with silver braid and wore a brace of six-guns strapped to his belt. Downtown merchants advertised special purchases of blue jeans and bandanas. This line of costuming suited me perfectly, for I generally ran around in cowboy clothes anyway, hoping to be mistaken for Tyrone Power in "Jesse James."

It had been the coldest February in decades — ten inches of snow on Mount Diablo, sleds on Skyline Boulevard and frozen goldfish ponds in Piedmont. Then, during the week, the cold wave broke, and the sun shone beguilingly on Metropolitan Oakland (also known in the *Tribune* as "Treasure Island's Mainland.") Leather vests and high-heeled boots were selling briskly at Capwell, Sullivan and Furth. The Orpheum was showing a four-reeler called "Fisherman's Wharf," starring Bobby Breen, Leo Carillo and Slicker the Seal. A dress designer brought out a Treasure Island wardrobe: the Coit Tower formal (a cylinder of pleated chiffon), the Lola Montez dress (a red organza bodice and a full skirt covered in black spider-web tracery), and the Fisherman's Wharf sports suit (oyster wool skirt, shrimp wool jacket and fishnet hat).

On the penultimate day of the Fiesta we wore cowboy hats and neckerchiefs to school, and they let classes out at noon. Three or four of us made a trek along Park Boulevard and down Excelsior, shooting cap pistols. On Grand Avenue there were facades of painted plywood on the dime stores, swinging doors, knot holes, hitching posts. "Red Eye, 15¢ — Black Eye, Free."

In a shop around the corner from the Grand Lake Theatre the neighborhood merchants were running a kangaroo court. They would haul in a man without whiskers and sentence him to hang unless he bought two tickets to the Welcome Cavalcade Ball in Municipal Auditorium, with music by Ben Pollack's Hollywood Orchestra and Don Mulford's University of California cowboy dance band.

I was not of beard-growing age and my father steadfastly refused to grow even a goatee. I saw this as a dereliction of civic duty for both of us, and I was apprehensive about the consequences. Bury me not on the lone prairie. Out on East 14th Street some service club zealots had pounced on a clean-shaven man who fought back, and three men came

out of it with knife wounds. My mother assured me I would not be forced to buy a ticket to Ben Pollack and Don Mulford if I walked down Lakeshore in dude clothes, but I figured those assurances would be useless with a rope around my neck. I knew the meaning of frontier justice. A mob of vigilantes at my school had held a kangaroo court on the playground and sentenced Joe Marion to five corks on the upper arm for burping without saying Safety-Toby-Watermelon. (It was his third offense — a born loser.)

Grand Avenue turned out to be less riotous than expected. Still, it vibrated with purposeful, premonitory energy — the sort of restless scurrying you see on a shopping street the afternoon before Christmas. There were firecrackers in the gutters and bins of paper mustaches along the sidewalk. The ladies at Woolworth's had on Spanish hats with ball fringe around the brims. The streetcars were wearing skirts of bunting. A sound truck passed: "I Sailed Away to Treasure Island." Steel guitars and ukuleles, a new motif. A breath of caramel corn, a whiff of gunpowder tweaked the air.

I was disarmed. What did it matter that Fiesta was a crass design, a municipal conspiracy to sell blue jeans and cowboy hats? Oakland is a town of willing boomers, suckled on false claims, exaggerations, bogus optimism. At dusk I walked home with a wad of pink bubblegum oozing sugar into my new molars and a rapture of expectation swelling in my throat.

The putative delights of the midnight carnival were not for me. I did not attend the Welcome Cavalcade Ball nor hear the concert of operatic arias by a thirteen-year-old soprano who called herself Leni Lynd, nor did I see the judging of the Whiskerino Contest by a bearded wrestler who called himself Rasputin. Not for me the giddy round of San Francisco, the dry martinis at Shanty Malone's, the sixty-five-cent, seven-course dinner (with wine) at Lucca's, the grand parade on Market Street.

It was enough to know such things existed and would be enjoyed (as I assumed they would be) by every adult within fifty miles. The newspapers convinced me that San Francisco had gone mad with ecstasy. Polk Street had literally become Polk Gulch. The foggy Sunset District had turned into El Rancho del Sol. Wild horses roamed in Sutro Forest; burro trains and mounted posses were converging on the city from every homestead in the West. Hundreds of thousands of insensate revelers, inflamed with "Exposition Fever" (as the papers called it) were poised to storm the gates of Treasure Island at daybreak.

64

Recently, it came as a surprise to me to learn that the sponsors of the Exposition had exactly the same impression as I did. I should have thought that those who invented and propagated the fever would have been immune to it. To the contrary, Leland Cutler and George Creel and other functionaries of Treasure Island were even worse infected than I was.

For weeks they had been entertaining selected groups of consular representatives, army and navy officers, foreign delegates and Chamber of Commerce committeemen on preview tours. The polite enthusiasm of the visitors, the sweet memories of 1915 and the ardent spirits of the Fiesta had begun to ferment their brains. They looked at the 12,000-car parking lot at the north end of the island and multiplied its capacity by five passengers a car. They thought about the great white fleet of passenger ferries wallowing across the bay from San Francisco at ten- or fifteen-minute intervals, and the endless orange caravan of Key Route electric trains, marked X for EXposition, rumbling toward the Oakland Mole from Berkeley, Piedmont and San Leandro. It was easy to calculate that there would be 175,000 — make it 200,000 — paying customers on opening day.

Cutler began to hallucinate. He envisioned an apocalyptic scene of bumper-to-bumper highways, battering rams at the ticket gates, ravening men and sobbing women thronging the Jolly Roger Hamburger Shop and the Oakwood Barbecue. He broadcast a radio announcement urging people to bring bag lunches and allow time for traffic jams. He warned them they had better plan to make a day of it.

My own claustrophobic family was grateful for the advice. We stayed home and ate bacon-lettuce-and-tomato sandwiches in the breakfast nook while Cutler's frustrated concessionaires awaited us, gnashing their teeth.

As Cutler recalled it later:

"Opening day was a beautiful one, and I paced up and down on the balcony and waited for the overflowing crowds. Even now I have a sinking feeling as my disappointment comes back to me . . . I was like a kid who looked forward to the picnic and the day of the picnic it rained and he didn't have any fun at all."

Cutler mislaid his top hat on the way to the opening ceremonies, Creel's speech was drowned out by a band playing "Home on the Range" and only 130,000 customers came through the turnstiles. Otherwise, the first day was a huge success.

The directors began the show with an electronic trick which showed, if nothing else, that they were sticking by the Pacific Basin. They arranged to have a photoelectric cell set up in Bombay, India, in a spot where it would catch the rays of the sun at exactly noon — 10:30 Friday night in San Francisco — and generate a radio signal across the Pacific. The radio signal flipped a switch at the Exposition, turned on the outdoor lights and prodded the carillon in the Tower of the Sun into a forty-four tone rendition of "The Bells of Treasure Island," one of several more or less official theme songs of the fair. Bakery drivers unloading hamburger buns at the food stands stopped and craned their necks in astonishment. Painters on scaffolds glanced at their watches and bellowed, "Get the lead out!" A friend of ours who was living on Telegraph Hill sprained her ankle in a rush to the window.

This unique demonstration of Pacfic unity continued to puzzle some of the customers throughout the Exposition. They kept writing letters to the management, asking whether it was true that the lights of Treasure Island were controlled from India.

At noon the next day, while the first paid customers were filtering through the wind baffles in the western wall, Governor Culbert Olson officiated at a traditional dedicatory ritual, opening the central span of a small replica of the Golden Gate Bridge with a jeweled key. The Governor had been sick in bed and was looking peaked, but the key was terrific. It was ten inches long, solid gold, with a Golden Gate Bridge of its own along the top, diamonds and tourmalines on the sides, and, here and there, enamel miniatures of the State Capital, Mission Santa Barbara and other scenes on the California tourist itinerary. Jewelers around the country had donated old lavaliers, brooches and earrings to be melted down. The jewelers' association priced the key at $35,000. Nobody seems to know what became of it.

The audience hung on for half an hour of band music and a broadcast from Key West, Florida, by President Roosevelt, who said it was a fine thing when a country could acquire a new island without aggression. Then, everyone fanned out into the courtyards and esplanades where all the flowers were freshly sprinkled and the loudspeakers were thumping out "Flat Foot Floogie with a Floy Floy," "Bei Mir Bist Du Schoen" and "Ferdinand, the Bull with the Delicate Ego."

College men in blue and gold uniforms and visored caps rushed forward, offering rides in rolling chairs and rickshaws, tours in Elephant Trains, maps of the island.

"You can't find your way around the fair without a guidebook. You'll get lost, lady. You'll get awfully, awfully, *awfully* lost, and you won't know where to turn . . . "

"Hey! Over here! Buy a ticket for the Elephant Train and get away from the noise . . . "

But the visitors wandered along in tight little groups, like shoppers exploring a grand bazaar, keeping hold of the children and occasionally nudging one another toward a bed of early tulips or an open door.

A few of the older people, remembering the haunted classicism, the refulgent domes and cloisters of the Panama-Pacific Exposition, were disappointed. Treasure Island suggested the past without recapturing it. The Tower of the Sun was no Tower of Jewels; the airplane hangar filled with European paintings was no Palace of Fine Arts. Nowhere was there that atmosphere of gentle melancholy that had suffused the dream city of 1915 like sunset gilding the Villa of Hadrian. A few of the young were disappointed, too, sensing that the false exoticism of the buildings reflected a nostalgic attachment to the past, a loss of nerve to face the future.

But hardly anyone voiced these disappointments. We were grateful that Treasure Island could exist, at all, in a world so constantly agitated by the drums and swords of hostile nations. The mere endurance of this fragile city, ringed around with dancing water, under clouds that rose like pewter plates behind the Berkeley hills, was reassurance against anxiety, reinforcing our sense of civic pride, our duty to extol the Exposition, overlook its faults and praise its virtues.

The key that officially opened Treasure Island was made of solid gold and set with benitoites, tourmalines, diamonds and enamel miniatures. Hundreds of jewelers contributed baubles to be melted and mixed into the confection.

Official Key to the GOLDEN GATE INTERNATIONAL EXPOSITION

67

68   *The causeway was packed with cars on Saturday morning,*
      February 18, 1939, but the size of the crowd dismayed the management.

THE OPENING—
SOMBREROS
AND BAG LUNCHES

Long before the fair was built, the founding fathers decided to open Treasure Island on February 18, the starting date of the 1915 Panama-Pacific Exposition. Later, when Treasure Island was in financial agony, no one could explain why it had seemed important to begin in mid-winter, when most Americans were at work or at school — but everyone agreed that February is a lovely month in San Francisco.

The weather, which had been cold and bleak, turned bright and breezy. Newspapers came out with glossy souvenir editions, and businessmen wore rodeo hats. For a wonderful moment it seemed that the flow of history had stopped, or shifted to the Yerba Buena Shoals — one auspicious moment, written in the stars, when everything, suddenly, seemed to be getting better.

Moppets modeled satin shirts
and cartridge belts outside
a haberdashery in the Sunset District.

Tourists on horseback, merchants in beards

For a week before the Exposition the Bay Area reveled in one of those costumed "fiestas" that were the hope and surcease of the Depression economy — the third or fourth occasion in as many years when it was practically mandatory to wear a plaid flannel shirt and blue jeans and get drunk at noon.

A public relations agency with a mimeograph machine turned out releases announcing the transformation of the Mission District into the Old Mission

Horseback posses from inland valleys cantered through San Francisco's business streets.

Trail and Chestnut Street into the Marina Coast. The Mayor wore a black Stetson, a bank put up a prize for beard-growing — and, before long, everyone was walking bowlegged and smoking Bull Durham.

Wagon trains set out from Sacramento: "Treasure Island or Bust!" Kangaroo courts persecuted clean-shaven male citizens. A lyricist turned out a number called "Gotta Getta Goin' to the Golden Gate to My Fair One at the Fair."

The result, in the words of an ecstatic publicity man, was "the greatest round of business-building ever staged by any city — a twenty-two percent jump in retail sales during the week!"

Bank President Parker S. Maddux, head of the Fiesta Committee, posed with toy pistol bandits in the interest of commercial recovery.

Raiders from Haight Street lynched Edgar Brownstone, a Polk Street merchant, to improve business conditions in both neighborhoods.

71

Opening Day patrons at the Ferry Building lined up to get exact change for the boat ride (ten cents each way). The Exposition Shoe Shine Shop, adjoining the change booth, was one of hundreds of Bay Area businesses that took a new name in honor of the fair.

The urge to be first

The instinct that drives climbers to the tops of mountains filled the eight o'clock ferry with adventurers determined to beat the rest of mankind to the new territory. These were the self-proclaimed charter patrons, the pioneers of Treasure Island — but they were fewer in number than exhibitors had hoped. President Leland Cutler, expecting 200,000 customers the first day, had warned people to leave their cars at home and bring along a bag lunch, and many took the warning as an invitation to stay away. Fewer than 130,000 appeared, and only 7,000 passed through the turnstiles the first hour.

74 *The 90-foot Arch of Triumph, tinted coral pink, looked like a monument to a conquering emperor, but it functioned mainly as a background for family photographs.*

Footsteps in a new world

First-day explorers walked every inch of the island, getting the sense of its vistas and spaces. Names that had become familiar in publicity stories took shape at last: the Tower of the Sun, the Court of the Moon, the statue of Pacifica — these were landmarks that would persist in memory long after the fair was gone.

The Court of the Seven Seas was distinguished by crow's-nest lamp posts and inordinate length — 1,000 feet from end to end.

To walk the island was one of the enduring pleasures of the Exposition. Often, it was an aimless, day-long stroll — across the Asian bridge that spanned a neck of the lagoon, along the asphalt Promenade of the Seven Seas, among the Irish yews and Ali Baba vases of the Court of the Moon. Much of the pleasure was in the freshness of the air and the unbelievable abundance of the flowers. There were, according to the meticulous Official Guide Book, 15,000 Jersey Gem violas, 37,125 white English daisies, 44,000 Amurense lemon-yellow poppies, 23,040 Dutch iris, 15,000 Bismark hyacinths — hundreds of thousands of flowers in every season.

Rodeo girls on motorcycles and college students in Harold Teen jalopies waited overnight for the toll gates to open. In the Gayway (left) there was an unscheduled parade of Opening Day fashions.

Serapes and rebozos from the Fiesta were ideal apparel if you didn't mind being stared at.

I must say, nobody had to sell the Exposition to *me*. During the week or two that passed before I had an opportunity to step onto the island, I suffered a six-month torment of anticipation. My mother went over one afternoon during the first week, wearing a navy blue polka dot dress and a hat attributed to Lily Daché, and came back, windblown and triumphant: she had *seen* Botticelli's "Birth of Venus."

I congratulated her, of course, although the art exhibit was not my idea of a primary target. My strategy was to sample *everything* on the first visit, as in a preliminary sweep of the smorgasbord at the Bit o' Sweden. Once I had separated the meatballs from the pickled herring, so to speak, I would go back for second helpings of the things I liked. But when my opportunity came at last, my feet got tired, notwithstanding a treatment at a Foot Comfort Station (a little platform that vibrated underfoot when you put a nickel in a slot), and I had to accept the philosophical position (always difficult for me) that there would be another day.

Altogether, there were dozens of other days. I savored most of the attractions of the Exposition, from the El Salvador Marimba Band to the Australian kangaroos, and repeatedly tried to extend my patronage to Sally Rand's Nude Ranch, which repeatedly turned me away. Still, I never felt that I had covered every possibility. Nor did I ever learn the proper names of all the courts and malls and palaces. I suspect that no one except the architects and the employees of the Exposition ever got hold of those geographic distinctions.

Every space on the island had a majestic name — Court of Honor, Court of the Seven Seas and so on. Clyde Vandeburg brought some of them from the San Diego Fair: lovely, second-hand names, mellow and soft with age, like rented costumes. Tower of the Sun was one of them. Ted Huggins, on loan from Standard Oil for such purposes, spent hours thinking up adjectives to drape on concourse, boulevard and esplanade. He wanted to call the western shore "The Bund," after the Shanghai waterfront, but had to change the name when people associated it with the Nazi Party.

The great courts differed in color and shape, of course, but they all flowed together, as the architects had intended them to do, so that you never felt compelled to say to yourself, "Well, well! Here I am in the Court of Reflections."

Only two courts had much distinction. One of them was called the Court of the Moon. It glowed at night with a supernatural azure light, known in the official pallette as "Evening Star Blue." At one end was Ettore Cadorin's statue "The Evening Star," standing on tiptoe, mother naked, on a pedestal surrounded by old apple trees and beds of blue hydrangeas. "The Evening Star" was the most popular statue on the island, and I, for one, thought it was probably the most beautiful representation of the female figure ever wrought by the hand of man.

The other distinctive place was the Court of Pacifica, a big roundabout with a cascading fountain in the center. The Court of Pacifica was the axis of the fair. It was always crowded with rickshaw pullers and bath-chair pushers, lost children, photographers-for-hire, old ladies in black cardboard sombreros and school tours from San Jose and Chico, mustering ranks for an assault on the free samples in the Food and Beverage Building.

Around the central fountain the designers had placed more than a dozen thick-limbed, pouty-lipped statues — Indian women hunkering over stone metates, Tehuantepec boys riding alligators, Inca girls playing flutes, Polynesians strumming ukuleles and other characteristic denizens of the Pacific Basin. Chunky, sleek and imperturable, these statues epitomized the style of the Exposition. Several of them resembled pre-Columbian artifacts from Central America. Others looked like the stone faces of Easter Island. A few, I think, were Cambodian.

There was a theory of demography, a mild political message implied in this congress of sculpture. Clustered together around the water, the figures testified to the existence of a mystical, physical, supra-political Pacific unity. Although everyone knew this unity had broken down in recent years, most Americans still accepted it as a worthy goal, and we were reassured to see all those primitive and heterogeneous foreigners fraternizing among the chrysanthemums. Pacific Basin, in other words, was more than a style — it was a moral statement, like the Century of Progress celebrated in Chicago in 1932 or the Brotherhood of Man promulgated in Montreal in 1967. I remember reading with approval (not amusement) that the Elephant Towers above the western gates were a perfect synthesis of Pacific traditions: "The pyramids have a Mayan

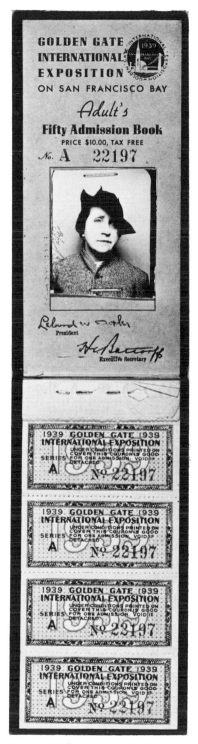

Season tickets carried photographs appropriate to passports, driver's licenses and police mug-books.

81

touch; the elephants show the influence of Burmese form; and the howdahs are distinctly Malayan."

This sort of commentary, pumped out by the press office, probably was meant to suggest that the towers were classic, if not immortal, but I don't think anyone took this aspect of it seriously. We Californians had a well-known weakness for kitsch architecture — fruit juice stands in the shape of mammoth oranges, brown derby restaurants, hot dogs in the sky — and we were as sure to like elephant-headed towers as we were to admire the giant cash register that recorded the daily attendance. I never knew anyone who was grossly offended by the architectural excesses of Treasure Island — the ogival windows, the Siamese pagodas, the crow's nest lamps, the rows of ships' prows creasing the air. We thought they were ingenious.

At least one imported architectural feature was brilliantly adapted to the uses of an exposition. It was a pair of giant stairways, or ghats, patterned after the river landings of India. (Pacific Basin could encompass India as comfortably as Persia or Burma.) The ghats overlooked the bandstand and the lagoon, and they were an ideal place to sit while eating corn on the cob and listening to Benny Goodman.

Professional critics were cool to Pacific Basin style. Most of them agreed with *Time* magazine that the Exposition was an "exotic chow-chow of the ageless East and the American West." Oswald Garrison Villard reported in *The Nation* that he was charmed by the island, but he went on: "It probably would commend itself little to Frank Lloyd Wright except as a tasteful continuation of the architectural past. It has not the bizarreness of the New York Fair, nor does it give such an impression of strength and power."

Only two or three buildings stirred the enthusiasm of the critical fraternity: William W. Wurster's finely textured Yerba Buena Club house, Timothy Pflueger's Federal Colonnade and William Gladstone Merchant's cruciform Pacific House. All were clearly at variance with the Indo-Malayan scheme.

As for the Tower of the Sun, the 400-foot campanile sticking up from the low horizon, hardly anyone could tolerate it. One critic likened it unfavorably to the Harkness Tower at Yale University — "a gothic lantern, capped by a candle-snuffer pinnacle." Herb Caen, the *Chronicle* columnist, called it "Egyptian style of the WPA dynasty," and Beniamino Bufano, the sculptor and artistic gadfly, said it should have been used as the minaret of a mosque. Even the broadly tolerant sculptor

82

Ralph Stackpole shrugged it off — "The thing is up — what can you do about it?"

Stackpole's own contribution to Pacific Basin style was a colossus called "Pacifica," an eighty-foot female figure of phlegmatic aspect and monolithic physique. "Pacifica" stood at the end of a magnificent corridor, like a set for a Cecil B. De Mille film about some defunct religion. Just behind her hung a network of metal disks that was supposed to quiver and tinkle in the Pacific breeze. The architects had been so successful in blocking wind at this point that they had to install electric fans to keep the Prayer Curtain moving.

Everybody liked "Pacifica," perhaps because of her eerie likeness to an overgrown automobile radiator ornament, and Ralph Stackpole considered her a masterpiece. A few years ago, when the city government of San Francisco was casting around for something to do with the island of Alcatraz, Stackpole suggested putting up a new "Pacifica" to counterpoise New York's Statue of Liberty. Nobody grabbed at the idea, but it was a poignant reminder that nothing remains to the public of the Golden Gate International Exposition but a few small sculptures, some murals and a peculiarly named naval base.

Few of us fair-goers cared what architectural critics thought of Treasure Island. If the architecture of our Exposition was conservative, it never was objectionable, whereas the theme buildings of the New York Fair — the massive geometric trylon and perisphere — were not only banal but suggestive. Around my junior high school, where the hot blood of local chauvinism ran in every vein, the trylon and perisphere were known as New York's You-Know-What, and they showed up in an astonishing variety of uses on the walls of the boys' room.

Only art critics and historians judge a world's fair by its architecture. Most people looked on the exhibit buildings merely as a pleasant setting for displays and restaurants, free pamphlets, take-home samples, inexpensive souvenirs. Long after the configuration of the walls had faded from my mind, the imprint of certain scenes remained: the Navajos at the Federal Building, laying out designs in colored sand; the collection of miniatures, culminating in a grain of rice with the Lord's Prayer inscribed on one side; the juggler on a unicycle, balancing on a tight wire dozens of feet above the asphalt paving of the Gayway.

84　　*The Court of Flowers, designed by Lewis P. Hobart, had Pacific Basin touches: Siamese umbrella lights, massive buttresses and arches and a Cambodian tower looming above — but O.C. Malmquist's "Girl and Rainbow" statue looked more Grecian than Pacific.*

THEY CALLED THE STYLE "PACIFIC BASIN"

Chunky, ham-handed figures in the Court of Pacifica symbolized peace and unity among native races of the Pacific.

Borrowed from Malaya, Indonesia and the ancient jungle cities of Cambodia and Yucatan, the architectural style of Treasure Island was a peculiar product of its times. Arthur Brown, Jr.'s committee of mellow, sixtyish beaux arts architects vowed to avoid the influence of contemporary fashion. Ignoring new materials and organic form, they invented a unique syncretistic style that had no past and no future. But history played them an ironic trick: with its laid-on grandeur and its nostalgia for traditional decoration, Pacific Basin style resembled the 1930s fascist architecture of Mussolini's Italy and Hitler's Germany.

Polynesian chieftan, Chinese musician and Mexican peasant were among the group of "Pacific unity" statues around the Fountain of Western Waters.

Wind baffles designed by Ernest E. Weihe formed the western entrance, majestically named Portals of the Pacific. Weihe worked with cardboard models, chicken feathers and electric fans to devise a system that would let people through the wall, keep breezes out.

Mayan-Burmese-Malayan Elephant Towers, designed by 26-year-old Donald Macky, flanked the main entrance. Lighted ruby-red by night, they were the goofiest, most distinctive feature of the fair. Some critics saw cubist influence, others detected a resemblance to wooden puzzle toys.

88

Court of the Seven Seas led to the Tower of the Sun. Sixteen bosomy, wing-spreading Spirits of Adventure looked down from the prows of ships, and Renaissance sea captains sailed over each doorway. The sculptures were by Haig Patigian, the architecture by George Kelham, and it was all in praise of exploration.

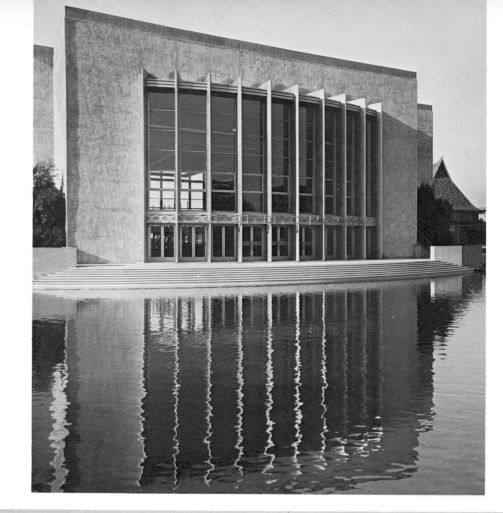

William Gladstone Merchant's Pacific House (left), the officially designated "Theme Building" of the Exposition, eschewed oriental gewgaws and won critical praise. Professionals also admired Timothy Pflueger's Federal Building (page 98) and W.W. Wurster's Yerba Buena Club (below) which were defiantly twentieth century in style. (At one of the Y.B. Club's Thursday fashion luncheons Du Pont introduced transparent Lucite shoes and a hair treatment called "Cellophane blonde." Some of the ladies thought things had gone entirely too far.)

Wherever you went on Treasure Island there always was someone lifting a baton to strike up the band, blowing a whistle to start a parade or grabbing a microphone to introduce the speaker-of-the-day. No excuse was needed to start a shivaree. Every honored guest, every politician in gestation, every actor with a film-in-can could bank on having an official day at Treasure Island. Gertrude Atherton and Gertrude Lawrence, Paul Bunyan and Paul Gallico, President Somoza and Gladys Swarthout, Lily Pons and Elsie the Cow — they all got in on it.

Quite unsuspecting, we customers would arrive at Treasure Island on a Saturday morning and be swept up in a flurry of name tags and forced marches, all in the interest of National Woman's Party Day, Insurance Day or Apple Day. The Thirtieth Infantry would be on the move, flags would be whipping horizontally above the Lagoon of Nations, and a few thousand shivering spectators would be huddled like penguins on the ghats, waiting for the speeches and the sopranos singing "Chiribiribin." There was no way to predict when girls in dirndls would be swarming over the island, handing out dried figs or Bartlett pears, and, equally, no way to predict when one might have the Court of Pacifica practically to himself.

One night in early June (it happened to be Public Wedding Day), nine loving couples said their marriage vows in the Court of Flowers. All the grooms wore navy blue jackets and white trousers. All the brides wore ankle-length white dresses and broad white picture hats. Mayor Rossi gave the brides away, en masse, and the carillon in the Tower of the Sun played Mendelssohn's "Wedding March."

I missed Public Wedding Day, and, for the life of me, I can't remember whether or not I joined the merry crowds on Wendell Willkie Day, Mantle Club Day or San Francisco Apartment House Industry Day. The Days had a way of getting lost, of melting into the events of those portentious years. Who can remember, for example, San Francisco Architectural Club Day? It fell on March 15, the day Adolf Hitler signed a protective treaty with President Emil Hàcha of Czechoslovakia and German soldiers in three-man motorcycles rolled into Prague.

Most of the special Days on Treasure Island were unabashedly commercial, like Ladies' Day at a baseball park. The management used them as an excuse to offer cut-rate gate passes to some organized segment of society, and the organized segments were delighted to slip in at a discount. In those days Americans had an insatiable craving for minor privileges and group field trips.

In this respect, as in all others, Treasure Island tried to conform to our tastes and habits. There was no television, of course, to shape our tastes and regularize our habits, but the papers and magazines made an effort to keep everyone in line with the latest social imperatives. About the time the Exposition opened, one of the San Francisco papers went to the trouble of interviewing a stylish young woman and publishing every one of her loves and hates. I have copied them down to suggest some of the attitudes of a typical crowd at Treasure Island on, say, Retail Furniture Day or Alpha Omicron Pi Sorority Day.

Loves

Off-the-shoulder formals
Cocktail parties
Black with silver fox
Travel to the Orient
The Rhumba
Charles Boyer
Daiquiris
Lake Tahoe
Dark red nail polish
Hawaiian music

Hates

Desserts
Flat-heeled shoes
Palm Springs
The waltz
Breakfast
Slinky formals
Cigars
Tennis
Carrots
Gin or wine

Even now, these prejudices strike me as quite reasonable, even endearing. When I consider that this young woman, multiplied by thousands, constituted what might be called the General Public of the Exposition, I am impressed anew with the qualities of that generation.

We were innovative: The Lucerne Dairy began selling milk (eleven cents a quart) in a new, no-return, waxed paper container, crimped at the top, with a lift and pour spout.

We were hospitable: Whenever Sir Cedric Hardwicke stopped at the

Mark Hopkins, Walter Pidgeon at the St. Francis or the Dead End Kids at the Empire, they got their names in the papers.

We were genuine: Pabst Blue Ribbon Beer had a *real* blue ribbon at the neck of every bottle.

We were fun: San Francisco society gave its daughters such names as Fritzi, Gwladys and Carmencita.

We were courageous: A new fashion in ladies' bathing suits — the strapless — coincided with the opening of the Exposition. A model in Los Angeles summed up our devil-may-care reaction: "Straps," she said, "are for streetcars."

We were wholesome: Every Sunday night at 8:30 we listened to "One Man's Family," the story of Mother and Father Barbour and Their Bewildering Offspring — Paul, Jack, Clifford, Claudia, Hazel and so on. They were all awfully nice and spent a lot of time giving each other advice and playing word games that involved Tenderleaf Tea.

We were discriminating: A cabal of milliners in New York tried to revive a medieval headdress called the wimple, which was well suited for hurricane weather around Cape Horn and pilgrimages to Canterbury, but it did not catch on.

We were progressive: An assemblyman from San Francisco introduced a bill in the Legislature to extend the closing hour of bars and liquor stores to 4 A.M. to help promote the Exposition.

We were virile: The best movie of the year was *Gunga Din*, with Victor McLaglen, Douglas Fairbanks, Jr., and Cary Grant. There was a woman in it, too, but nobody could remember her name. Anita Louise?

We were friendly: A seventeen-year-old waif named Brenda Diana Duff Frazier, who was beautiful, wore white satin gowns trimmed with ostrich feathers and had $4,000,000, made her debut in New York City, and we took her to our hearts.

About the only subject upon which we showed a grave insensitivity was popular music. Most of our music was entirely too popular. During the early months of the fair, a lifer in the Kansas State Penitentiary killed another prisoner who refused to stop whistling "Three Little Fishes," but Kay Kyser and his Kollege of Musical Knowledge came to Treasure Island, performed the fatal number at the Hall of Western States and escaped without being harmed.

RED-LETTER DAYS
FOR COMMONERS
AND KINGS

When the Maharajah of Karputhala visited Treasure
Island in May, 1939, with a pouch of jewels strapped
to his wrist and a gold-headed cane gripped firmly
in his hand, U.S. Commissioner George Creel and
British Consul Geoffrey Butler put on full dress and
white gloves, and the Thirtieth Infantry fired a
fifteen-gun salute.

   Not every visitor could count on such a reception,
but nearly everyone had a day to call his own. There
were Catholic Days and Jewish Days, Twin Days and
Freckle Days, days for showing off ancestral costumes
and — most happily — days for getting through
the gate free.

To the delight of the press room, Betty Barnes, the millionth customer, turned out to be a working-girl Cinderella who had come with only carfare and a bag lunch. Showered with passes and flowers, she grabbed more newspaper space than the Queen of the Nudists, whose transbay swim flopped that morning when the water proved cold and the cameramen ran out of film.

Also on hand: The 27-millionth Ford motor car.

Dozens of kids with more talent in their little finger than Shirley Temple had in her whole body showed up at a Chrysler Corporation Talent Search.

On a June evening in the Court of Flowers, Philip McKeon, Patrick Colgan, Hershel Bean, Robert Alexander, James Robinson, Robert Eaton, H.P. Yeary, Gordon Cusick and Joseph Sunscri married Loretta Ballard, Claire Davis, Eva Peterson, Maxine Kranwinkle, Edna Mae Steenton, Irene Ridge, Murguerite O'Brien, Bernice Sheldon and Laura Fachnie, respectively. Mayor Angelo Rossi gave the brides away.

Navy marching teams passed the 48-column Federal Building as the ubiquitous U.S. Commissioner George Creel watched in person and from the wall, where his face appeared on the body of a pneumatic drill operator in a WPA mural.

Boy Scouts in broad-brimmed Baden-Powell hats and khaki knickers marched down the Court of the Seven Seas on Scout Day. Later, boatloads of traffic boys took over.

Pacifica wore a recruit's cap on Navy Day, 1940.

The care and feeding of celebrated people

For the official hosts, there was no end to the cookie-pushing. Leland Cutler stood by with roses while Gertrude Lawrence, the British actress, played an unconvincing gardening scene in the Court of the Moon. George Creel served tea and ladyfingers to the family of Chief Big Turnip. And still the onslaught continued . . .

Former President Hoover (with Mrs. Hoover and Maj. Charles Kendrick) addressed an engineers' luncheon.

New York's Mayor LaGuardia paid his own way, warned San Francisco's Rossi he'd have to do the same at the New York Fair.

Ventriloquist Edgar Bergen played straightman to his dummy, Charlie McCarthy.

Comedian Eddie Cantor, after parting with four bits for two tickets, played a gig at a Guess-Your-Weight booth. The regular guesser confessed afterward: "I was telling him the weights in Yiddish."

On Sebastopol Day councilmen and cowboys took over
the Redwood Empire Building to sing the praises of Gravenstein apples.

Sciot drill teams and Indian Guides frequented the Federal Building.

102

With five girls in bunny bows and Carioca dresses, you could publicize practically anything, including this enticing event, the name of which is anybody's guess.

An exuberant drum major named Maxine Turner led the San Leandro High School Pirate Band in a concert at the Alameda-Contra Costa Building. The occasion: San Leandro Schools Day.

104   *Pale virgins in white gowns and trolls in crepe paper
shawls gave the May Day procession a distinctly pagan look.*

Flag Day exercises were bouncy
and gymnastic, as were Treasure
Island's frequent band parades.

It was the hundredth anniversary of baseball — just the sort of historic event they loved to celebrate at Treasure Island — and the San Francisco Seals, of the erstwhile Pacific Coast League, sent their catcher, Joe Sprinz, over to the Island for a jazzy demonstration of long-ball fielding.

There was a sort of world record at stake. A man in Ohio had caught a ball dropped 758 feet from the top of the Terminal Tower in Cleveland. Sprinz figured to better that by nailing one tossed from the Goodyear blimp "Volunteer," hovering 800 feet above the field.

The first drop fell into the stands, where 1,200 fans screamed and covered their heads. The second hit the field like a cannonball and buried itself six inches in the turf. The third was right to Sprinz, but the sun got in his eyes.

They carried Sprinz to the hospital with a bashed nose, torn lips and four teeth knocked out of his dental bridge.

"Boy," said Sprinz, "I thought the blimp fell on me."

We liked our theatrical entertainments massive and repetitious, with plenty of synchronized dances, changes of costume and fluorescent lighting. The cult of Florenz Ziegfeld still had a firm grip on the music halls of New York, and Busby Berkeley commanded the staircases of Hollywood. Their local imitators set up a stage outside the Federal Pavilion where young women marched to and fro with open parasols while cadets saluted and sopranos in wide-brimmed hats sang "God Bless America."

One afternoon, rounding the lagoon, I caught sight of the afternoon show in progress. I quick-stepped past the California State Building to have a look at it, but the performance came to a sudden climax of whirling umbrellas and close-order drill before I could get there. By the time I panted up to the empty stage, the musicians were packing up and the audience had wandered off toward the ghats in search of a free band concert. We liked our show-biz fast-moving, too.

The biggest show on Treasure Island was a boots-and-saddle pageant called in 1939 *Cavalcade of the Golden West* and in 1940 *America! Cavalcade of a Nation.* Under either name it was roughly the same thing

— a succession of crowd scenes on an outdoor stage two-thirds as long as a football field, with a range of painted mountains as a backdrop and 2,500 lighted water jets as a front curtain. For fifty cents admission (twenty-five cents for children) you could be eyewitness to several dozen of the significant moments of Western history, omitting the Chinese Exclusion Act, the Central Pacific Refunding Bill and the San Francisco Red Light Abatement Act of 1914. Art Linkletter, who was at that time an interviewer on a radio station in San Francisco, wrote the script. In both years it was strong on flag-raisings and treaty-signings, weak on plot and character development. In both years it had more grand marches than a Meyerbeer opera. And in both years it was the primary "family show" on the island.

Some neighbors of ours reported that their evening at the Cavalcade was the most bone-chilling experience they had endured since they gave up going to Easter sunrise services in Cragmont. On their advice, we saw the Cavalcade (for the first time) by day. But the sky, the buildings, the Giant Crane and roller coaster off in the distance intruded on the scenery, diminishing the pageant. At night, with a murky bank of seafog for a proscenium arch, the Cavalcade was more believable. I was quite swept up in the illusion that American history consisted of a series of immense outdoor rallies, with crowds of men and women shouting "The Redcoats are coming!" or "Yay, Santy Ana!" or "On to Oregon!"

As for the ravages of the weather, they were really no worse than you might encounter any night at Seals' Stadium. The management rented out pillows and blankets to fortify the audience for the rigors of the Westward Expansion, and many adults also brought along invigorating little Thermos jugs of coffee laced with brandy. I was denied that tonic, of course, on grounds that children did not need it, and I have wondered whether the performers also had to meet the demands of Manifest Destiny night after night without stimulation.

The Cavalcade employed two sets of actors: an indoor cast of nine and an outdoor cast of 300. The indoor cast read the lines into loudspeakers while the outdoor cast signed treaties and raised flags. Outnumbered more than thirty to one, the indoor cast made up for its handicap by reading 100 roles, while the outdoor cast played 2,000 roles. (Frequent changes of costume probably helped them ward off chilblains.) In spite of this doubling of roles, the action, so to speak, was always perfectly clear. The speaker was the one who was waving his arms, and an announcer explained what everyone else was doing.

Grand finale at Federal Plaza brought dancers downstage in a farewell salute.

I suppose the Cavalcade was pretty terrible, what with all those polled Hereford steers posing as Texas longhorns, those trains and stagecoaches rolling slowly across the stage while a handful of radio actors shouted into a microphone. The lines were by no means national monuments of literature. ("To California's treasure-laden hills come rich man, poor man, beggar man, thief . . . ")

But our standards were indulgent. There was no Disneyland, no Marine World, no Las Vegas to satiate our native taste for large-scale marvels. Only the parking lot collected more money than the Cavalcade. I happily paid my quarter several times to see the cattle drive, the gold rush and the can-can in a turn-of-the-century saloon, and I was proud that the same Western tableaux reappeared in 1940 in *The Cavalcade of a Nation*, along with the siege of the Alamo, the composing of "The Star Spangled Banner," George Washington's winter at Valley Forge, the founding of Jamestown, the Boston Stamp Act riot and the midnight ride of Paul Revere. Like many Westerners, I worried that "our" history was somehow less significant than that of the established East, and I welcomed reassurance.

During the first year of the fair, there was practically no other pageant to compete with the Cavalcade. The *Folies Bergère* departed for Los Angeles. A Jake Shubert production called *Ziegfeld Follies of 1939*, which purposed to charm the masses with numbers entitled "Jitterbugs in the Jungle," "Swing Open the Golden Gate" and "Howja Like to Kiss Me Goodnight?" lasted only a few weeks before doing what *Variety* termed "el foldo." Meanwhile, to the anguish of the Exposition management, the *Ice Follies* opened to full houses in San Francisco. Dozens of other shows and concerts were luring customers away from the island — Marian Anderson, Paul Hindemith, even Trudi Schoop's Comic Ballet.

Fortunately, the *Folies Bergère* came back — a "new" *Folies Bergère*, replete with sequins and marabou capes and xylophones and advertisements that no healthy boy of twelve or thirteen could resist.

"Four thousand glamorous young ladies auditioned in Paris, London and New York for the current production," the program said. "All are breath-takingly beautiful."

From the twenty-eight-cent seats it was difficult to tell whether the glamorous young ladies were naked or clothed, much less what they looked like. But I can testify that the show was worth your twenty-eight cents (or even your fifty-five cents or eighty-three cents, if you happened to be prodigal). There was a celebrated flesh-and-the-devil scene—claws, horns, gilded bodies and erogenous nuzzling — that was the talk of our eighth grade; and, with field glasses, you could see that many of the mannequins who were prancing around, shedding ostrich plumes on the spiral staircase, were substantially naked. (Cynics of my acquaintance said they had on skin-colored tights, but in such matters it is the visceral feelings of the viewer that count, and my viscera felt that flesh was in view.)

In our household the *Folies Bergère* did not qualify as family entertainment, and I did not attend it with my family. As a matter of fact, my family was under the impression that I did not attend it at all. My family liked to think I spent long afternoons absorbing the secrets of the salamander embryo at the University of California science exhibit. They would have been surprised by my taste for xylophone music and breath-takingly beautiful young ladies.

During the early months of the Exposition, I always went over to Treasure Island with my mother and father, who stood treat and graciously allowed me to take snapshots of them lending scale to the buildings. After I turned twelve, however, and asserted a right to travel alone on the Key System, I often went on Saturdays or holidays with friends. It was in the company of a cousin from the Middle West that I first made it into the *Folies Bergère*. My cousin was fourteen and had a valuable card that identified him as a graduate student at the University of Kansas. Later that day I threw up while riding the Giant Octopus, but even that indignity did not diminish my sense of precocious maturity — nor have I ever lost my affection for the ticket seller who (repeatedly) mistook me for an eighteen-year-old, although I was obviously in the throes of vilest puberty.

(One of my friends, suffering from the same organic condition, was taken by his parents to an evening performance of the *Folies*. They hoped to satisfy his expressed curiosity about certain types of adult entertainment, as well as to impress him with their tolerance. In order not to disappoint them, he pretended he had never seen the show before, but he went too far by suggesting that the whole family come back for a repeat performance some afternoon when the prices were lower.)

Many of the best shows on Treasure Island were free. After blowing twenty-eight cents for a couple of hours of nudism and xylophone music, we would stop by at the Levi Strauss marionette rodeo or wander over to the Federal Building to take in the Hansel and Gretel puppet show. Edwin Franko Goldman's brass band played Sousa marches on the shore

Folies Bergère *performers dressed up in the dressing rooms, molted onstage.*

of the lagoon. Later, when the Exposition management decided that sort of music was passé, Eddie Duchin, Duke Ellington, Count Basie and Benny Goodman came to the bandstand at the ghats.

Only one show set a new style, however, and that one was the *Aquacade*, water ballet in a huge indoor pool. Billy Rose, the impressario, had originated the *Aquacade* in Cleveland and presented it at the New York World's Fair in 1939, where it attracted 5,000,000 spectators. In 1940 a West Coast production of the same show was the financial honey at Treasure Island.

The *Aquacade* was the pattern for uncountable amateur water carnivals in summer camps and country clubs across America. Every teenaged boy who saw it was inflamed with ambition to become an acrobatic Aquadope and hurtle himself off the high tower, dressed in baggy trousers, ruptured suspenders and a crimson fright wig, frozen in a grotesque one-legged dive, missed gainer, screaming belly-flop or super cannonball. This ambition showed up all summer long at Pinecrest, Twain-Harte and other places in my social radius, and sometimes it carried through the winter at the Athens Club and the Hayward Plunge. It must have affected every body of fresh water in North America.

Then, too, there was the *Aquacade* synchronized windmill swimming style: one stroke overhand, one backstroke, one stroke overhand, one backstroke, and so on. We practiced it in the lakes of the Sierra, counting aloud to stay together. The windmill stroke always made me dizzy, and I have never understood how Esther Williams kept her head on, swimming around the tank that way, three shows a day, four on Saturday and Sunday.

Esther Williams was the star of the *Aquacade*. The sports pages, I am sorry to say, sometimes called her the "prima swimeuse." She was eighteen and had won the National AAU 100-meter freestyle championship the year before. Publicity materials emanating from the office of the *Aquacade* described Miss Williams as a "typically healthy, alert, vibrant, cultured American girl," but if you think I fell for that you are underestimating the worldliness of thirteen-year-old boys. I figured Miss Williams was a sex machine, like all actresses, and raised the temperature of the water twenty degrees.

There was nothing about Miss Williams or her performance in the *Aquacade* to justify this fantasy. Her entire role, as I remember it, consisted of slithering round and round the pool in that vertiginous windmill swimming style while Morton Downey ("The Golden Voice of Radio") sang "I'm yoooours . . . for a sonnnnnng . . . for a sonnnng of romannnnce . . ." Miss Williams dove without splashing, swam without snorting and smiled angelically, even under water. No marabou capes, no messing around with slippery-fingered satyrs in gold lamé tights. Every bit of it was the sort of entertainment I could recommend to my parents. The Aquabelles and Aquabeaux were decently clad in sateen bathing suits and fluorescent rubber caps. The Aquafemmes (non-swimmers) minced around the water's edge like girls keeping their hair dry on the day of a country club dance. They wore Coney Island surfing clothes of the Teddy Roosevelt period.

The "Number One Aquadonis" was Johnny Weissmuller, the Tarzan of countless motion pictures. He had long hair, a muscular physique and a vocation for underwater wrestling. The *Aquacade* did not afford him any opportunity to grapple with alligators, and he looked a little restless confined to a seventy-two-degree indoor tank, surrounded by dancing Aquagals and backed up by Fred Waring's Glee Club singing "Yankee Doodle's Gonna Go to Town Again" over the plashing of the chlorinated waves.

That was the grand finale, the Yankee Doodle scene. Billy Rose put it at the end to send the customers away whistling. It stayed in your head, all right — a swirl of red, white and blue flags and chesty swimmers with their chins up, like a standing retort to the pacifist speeches that Kathleen Norris and other literary people were making over at the Temple of Religion, saying America should stay out of Europe's wars. I don't know how many people listened to Kathleen Norris, but I understand 25,000 saw the *Aquacade* the first day.

The reader may feel I have lingered too long and lovingly over these popular entertainments, none of which was a monument in theatrical history. If so, I apologize. It is a habit we all got into during the Exposition — because, of course, everyone went to the *Aquacade*, the *Cavalcade* and the *Folies Bergère*, and everyone wanted to talk about them, to savor again the excitement and laughter. Visitors from distant places were trotted over to the island, where reporters waited around with pencils poised to note down every gladsome outcry. Louella Parsons, the Hollywood columnist, spent the day and then reported with her usual ebullience: "Johnny Weissmuller, Esther Williams and Morton Downey are the biggest 40 cents worth of entertainment I ever saw."

112　*Temple Compound, outdoor showplace for big bands, overlooked
　　the Lake of the Nations.*

PAGEANTS ON
LAND AND WATER

Playing Treasure Island was a show-business equivalent of ordeal by freezing. The customers were tight with their two bits; repeaters were rare; and brassy all-girl villages that packed 'em in at Dallas and Cleveland withered and died in San Francisco. What they liked on Treasure Island was something big and beautiful and free, like Count Basie or Benny Goodman in an outdoor concert. Bing Crosby drew 60,000 to the amphitheater called Temple Compound on a Sunday afternoon in October — 22,500 seated on the benches and staircases and the rest standing shoulder-to-shoulder along the shore of the lagoon, with one enterprising kid up in a bamboo tree.

Smart showmen survived with glittery, low-priced pageants — Clifford Fischer's Folies Bergère, Adolph Vollman's two Cavalcades, Billy Rose's Aquacade. But even Jake Schubert's Ziegfeld Follies folded in the cool climate of the Yerba Buena Shoals.

Pianist Eddie Duchin followed the Treasure Island successs formula: keep it short, fast-moving and free.

300 actors and a herd of cows

Whether they called it the Cavalcade of the Golden West, as they did in 1939, *or the Cavalcade of a Nation,* as they did in 1940, *it was pretty much the same show — covered wagons, steam locomotives, soldiers on horseback and a stampede of polled Herefords under a painted backdrop of the High Sierra. They put on three performances a day (four on weekends) on a stage 400 feet wide and 200 feet deep, with a front curtain of water jets that sprayed thirty feet high.*

Everything about the Cavalcade was big, from the cast (300 human beings, 200 animals) to the loudspeakers that transmitted the voices of nine radio actors in 200 speaking roles.

"At a distance it's all right," one critic said. "Up close, it gives the effect of mass ventriloquism."

114

Rose called his synchronized swimmers "Aquabelles" and "Aquabeaux." Solo swimmers included Johnny Weissmuller and Channel swimmer Gertrude Ederle.

A master showman's wonderful water carnival

Billy Rose brought his Aquacade to Treasure Island in 1940 with the confidence of a ringmaster calling in the elephants. He had written hit songs ("That Old Gang of Mine," "Without a Song") and produced hit shows (Jumbo, Casa Mañana, Diamond Horse-shoe Review) and he knew exactly what the public wanted. The Aquacade was Rose at his best: schmaltzy music, slapstick comedy and pretty girls. Socko!

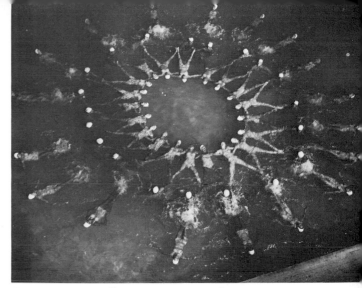

Swimmers wore fluorescent caps and swam intricate patterns in their black light scene.

Esther Williams, an 18-year-old amateur champion, went on to a movie career as an amphibious actress.

Dancing "Aquagals" in stars and stripes formed a tableau as the Fred Waring Glee Club sang "Yankee Doodle's Gonna Go to Town Again."

A friend of mine who was assigned by one of the San Francisco newspapers to daily duty on Treasure Island told me recently that he and his colleagues never considered writing a disparaging article about the fair. As newspapermen, they sensed a civic duty to exalt this local enterprise, which was providing diversion and employment for many of their kind.

I can testify that it was easy for a reporter to lapse into this sort of provincial flummery, because I happened to be a newspaperman myself during the early months of the fair. I was owner, publisher, circulation manager and co-editor of the *Night Hawk,* a weekly paper that Dared to Tell the Truth about events on Treasure Island's Mainland. My co-editor was Ken Wemmer. Ken wrote the stamp column, among other things, and drew the cartoons. I like to think he also was to blame for the typography.

The *Night Hawk* sold for ten cents a month. If you were lucky enough to get a copy that had been printed before the purple ditto ink began sinking into the hectograph jelly, it was well worth the price. There were poems, jokes, serialized novels, reviews of the latest films (*You Can't Take It with You* and *Son of Frankenstein*) and words of advice to the lovelorn. ("Just send in $.02 in coin for our new book on Love Problems.") In every issue we ran snappy articles, full of thrills, that Aunt Elsie would have given her last pencil box to print.

Like other periodicals in the Bay Area, the *Night Hawk* was slavishly devoted to the success of the Exposition. Our very first issue, which came out in the midst of the Whiskerino Contest, carried a weather report predicting "Cool today, Fair the 18th." From that date until the *Night Hawk* hibernated for the summer, we mentioned the Exposition in every issue.

(Incidentally, we were not alone in punning on "fair." Ann Corio, the striptease dancer, capitalized on Grover Whalen's decision to forbid nudity at the New York World's Fair by picketing Flushing Meadows with a sign that read: "World's Fair Unfair to World's Fairest Bodies." She got into *Life* magazine with that one.)

Among the *Night Hawk's* fiction serials was one about a family named Jones whose car broke down while crossing Arizona on the way to Treasure Island. (They may have been coming from Oklahoma; I don't remember.)

" 'This is a fine state of affairs, I must say,' said Mr. Jones. 'Here we are in the middle of the desert without any gas or drinking water!'

"At that moment a Navajo happened by on mule-back. Leveling a rifle on Our Friends, he said: 'Ugh! You not try to get away. Me want you for Trible Sacrafice!' (Continued next week.)"

The readers of the *Night Hawk* never learned whether the Jones family wound up being passed over the prairie. We dropped this fantasy of aboriginal life in Darkest Arizona in favor of a column called "Fair Fellow," which purported to be an objective report on exhibits-of-interest but was actually hard-sell for the Exposition. "Fair Fellow" was alternately Ken and I. We flacked blatantly on behalf of the Mines, Metals and Machinery Building, the Federal Theater, the Australian Building and the Pacific House. ("There are four sets of peep shows, two of which are modern art, and the other two which are sensible. Don't miss them.")

This kind of advocacy leads inevitably to corruption. In our April 7 issue "Fair Fellow" was mesmerized by the Hills Bros. Coffee Company's Exposition Theater.

The review occupied one quarter of a page. Under it was a quarter-page advertisement for Hills Bros. Coffee. It was the largest and most expensive advertisement that ever appeared in the *Night Hawk*. It cost the advertiser fifty cents, and he bought a piece of my soul in the bargain.

In gathering material for the "Fair Fellow" column, I made no distinction between purely commercial and putatively educational exhibits. To the contrary, my favorite beat was the Food and Beverages Building. I often lunched there on sample servings of Junket custard and Rancho Soup, inhaling fumes of roasted coffee wafted from a ventilator at Hills's Theater. I have kept a green plastic, pickle-shaped lapel pin from the Heinz exhibit and a "Where's Elsie?" badge from Borden's Milk. Every year these artifacts grow more precious, like Roman coins.

Near the center of the Food Building was a 1,000-pound fruitcake, whipped up by one Bill Baker of Ojai, California, out of 50 dozen eggs, 60 pounds of butter, 100 pounds of flour, 200 pounds of raisins, 150 pounds of citrus peel, 75 pounds of candied cherries and 10 gallons of sherry. It had a relief map of the Bay Area on top and 19 of the 21 California missions sculpted into the sides. On a solemn day in October, towards the end of the '39 fair, they chopped the whole thing into several thousand pieces and fed it to the hungry multitude.

All around the fruitcake, like side dishes on a buffet, were the food displays — raisin-packing machinery, a Coca-Cola bottling plant, a salt refinery, a kitchen where women in white caps dipped See's candies in milk chocolate — and a colony of live chinchillas in an air-conditioned glass case, set up to demonstrate the marvels of modern refrigeration.

If this sounds like the hall of commerce at a county fair, you have the right idea. Still, I found it difficult to tear myself away from such enticements. Most people my age, I am sorry to say, remember Heinz's free baked beans better than they do the Hall of Fine and Decorative Arts — but, of course, the art gallery cost a dime.

My own second choice, after Food and Beverages, was the Communications Building, where you could walk past a television camera that transmitted your image on a closed circuit to a receiving set in the next room. In the same building Bell Telephone raffled off a free long distance call every half hour, the hitch being that both ends of the conversation were broadcast to the passing crowd. A friend of mine won the raffle and to his embarrassment could not think of anyone to call. He settled on an aunt in San Jose. The call was answered by the aunt's Japanese gardener, who could speak only a few words of English. The whole episode reminded me of the woman who got three wishes and ended up with a string of link sausages attached to her nose.

The phone company also showed off a machine it had invented and named the Voder, an acronym for "Voice Operation Demonstrator." The Voder was a set of electrical vocal chords, played with a twenty-three-stop keyboard. It had a range of sssh's and m-m-m's and groans from basso profundo to coloratura, and a slight speech impediment — it said "les" instead of "yes." The phone company had trained several dozen operators to play the Voder, and they all said "les." According to these keyboard artists, the Voder had important secret uses beyond entertaining people at Treasure Island. I have sometimes wondered what they were. It is said that the Voder was a parent, technologically speaking, of a talking computer in the science fiction film *2001*. This would indicate the family stayed in show biz.

In the Communications Building, as in almost every exhibit hall, there were dozens of dioramas — large glass cases filled with figurines and miniature landscapes. Diorama was a word I had never heard before. (In the *Night Hawk* we called them peep shows.) But a few visits to Treasure Island made every neophyte an expert in the genre. We saw dioramas of business and industry, commerce and agriculture, history and science; dioramas of ski slopes, copper mines, college campuses, lumber mills and summer resorts.

Kevin Wallace, who wrote about Treasure Island every day in the *Examiner*, was astonished by the profusion of dioramas.

"Most of them are landscape effects, some industrial, and a few are

HEARING

TEST

USING MUSICAL TONES

In this test you listen through a telephone receiver. After spoken instructions you hear musical tones, all the same pitch, which come in groups, one, two, or three at a time. Successive groups sound farther and farther away. Each time you are to write the number of tones you heard. (The correctness of your record will measure your hearing for that pitch of tone.) Then you are tested in the same way for four other pitches. Your entire record forms a basis for rating your hearing.

BELL TELEPHONE EXHIBIT

GOLDEN GATE
INTERNATIONAL EXPOSITION
1939

sort of scientific slot machines, such as the University of California's heredity and anthropology dioramas, operated by push buttons. We are amazed there are suddenly so many dioramas in the world — and we wonder what diorama artists do in the lean years between expositions."

Wallace never got a satisfactory answer to the question. He continued to report on manifestations of the art, however, including a dioramic view of San Francisco in 1999, which the artist Donald McLoughlin had prepared for the United States Steel exhibit in the Hall of Mines, Metals and Machinery. This prognostic nightmare showed the city stripped of every vestige of 1939 except the Coit Tower, the bridges and Chinatown. All maritime activity had disappeared from the Embarcadero. Shipping was concentrated at a super-pier at the foot of 16th Street.

North of Market Street every block contained a single, identical high-rise apartment house. South of Market, sixty-story office towers of steel and glass alternated with block-square plazas in a vast checkerboard pattern. Elevated freeways ran through the geometric landscape. Subways and landing strips appeared at regular intervals. All in all, it looked uncomfortably tidy and overbearing, and Wallace feared the human race would have to be abolished if the World of Tomorrow was to work out according to the expectations of US Steel.

"There is something to be said for the future," he concluded, "and that is that any thoughtful consideration of it makes one glad to be living back here in the good old days."

Murals, machinery displays and dioramas are the sort of material that quickly evaporates from one's mind. The only diorama that permanently impressed me was Jo Mora's cavalcade of Spanish soldiers in the California Building, and that is probably because I had a poster of Indians by the same artist in my bedroom. The figures in Mora's diorama were struggling along through a bleak landscape of scrub brush and stunted pines, toward some rendezvous with imperial destiny. While you stood there watching, the lighting changed from dawn to noon to sunset, and a voice from a loudspeaker boomed out particulars of the Spanish conquest of Western America.

Having refreshed my memory by looking at a guidebook to the fair, I know that the scene represented Gaspar de Portola's expedition into upper California in 1769 and that the whole thing was destroyed by a fire that ruined the building on August 24, 1940. So far as I know, the figures were never recast, although the original molds were saved.

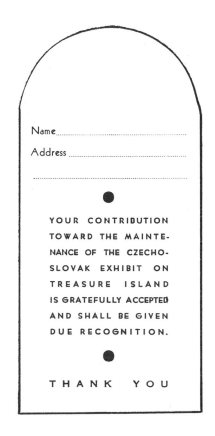

Name

Address

●

YOUR CONTRIBUTION TOWARD THE MAINTENANCE OF THE CZECHOSLOVAK EXHIBIT ON TREASURE ISLAND IS GRATEFULLY ACCEPTED AND SHALL BE GIVEN DUE RECOGNITION.

●

THANK YOU

PICKLE PINS
AND DIORAMAS

On any normal afternoon an energetic visitor could collect a shopping bag of information on vacation trips and cold-rolled steel, water softeners and business machines. The Exposition boasted that it opened the minds of children and enriched the lives of adults, and most of the opening and enriching was entrusted to exhibitors — large corporations (Bethlehem Steel, Dow Chemical, General Electric) neighboring states (Nevada, Arizona, Oregon) foreign powers (Johore, French Indochina, Netherlands East Indies) and friendly institutions (Girl Scouts, Lutherans, Lions).

Some of it was heavy. ("Spin a large coin in the dish below. Like the petroleum dollar you spend at your service station, it never stops circulating.") Some of it was dull. ("Gazing at the wonderfully detailed relief map of New Salem, Illinois, a feeling of reverence will come to you . . . ") But where else on earth could one obtain so much free literature on Du Pont nylon, Guatemala, and Christian Science?

Pacific Gas & Electric offered a free lecture and demonstration of the latest thing in utility billing machinery.

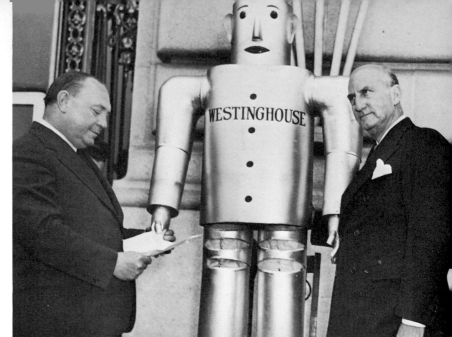

Westinghouse robot "Willie Vocalite" (seen here with O.J. Keatinge of the fair and San Francisco's Health Director J.C. Geiger) could sit down, stand up, talk and smoke cigarettes.

Along with the translucent Pontiac, General Motors displayed diesel automobile engines, the coming thing in Detroit in 1939.

Pacific House had an oceanic relief map, rattan furniture and the best original art at Treasure Island: Miguel Covarrubias's six mural maps of the culture and economy of the Pacific Basin.

This handsome South American exhibit took on special charm when printers left a key accent off the word maté in official guidebooks and advertised: "Be our guests at Cafe-Brazil, where you may sip Brazilian coffee or mate amid restful tropic surroundings."

THE
VODER
A
BELL
TELEPHONE
EXHIBIT

THE
VODER
A
BELL
TELEPHONE
EXHIBIT

"Pedro the Voder," a creature of the Bell Telephone Laboratories, was a keyboard-operated talking machine. He had a mild speech impediment but got laughs with snappy repartee.

The petroleum industry, heavy-handed as ever, erected a "Treasure Well" that offered a $1,000 prize to the person who could guess the total of next month's gasoline taxes. Some of the visitors succumbed to ennui.

Tour group inspecting a diorama of the Russian River had volunteer guidance from Zoe Dell Lantis, who bestrode Rio Nido like a colossus.

Telephone of the future, like much else at the fair, was transparent.

Spectators could get close to ceramicists using the potter's wheel, but most artists worked inside a fenced pit (below) while viewers watched them from a respectful distance.

Rivera's mural combined Mexican serpent-god Quetzalcoatl with modern machinery and glimpses of the Golden Gate Bridge and Treasure Island.

Rivera spent long hours on a scaffold above the hall, munching French bread while working.

A lively scene of art in the making

To replace the $40,000,000 collection of Old Masters shipped back to Europe after the first year, the Palace of Fine and Decorative Arts installed a brilliantly successful sideshow of sculpture, painting, weaving and pottery-making called "Art in Action."

A leading attraction was the Mexican muralist Diego Rivera, painting a huge fresco for the library of San Francisco City College. His close competitor was Ruth Cravath, who used live horses as models for a stone carving.

Out of "Art in Action" came granite statues, reliefs and paintings that now adorn San Francisco buildings and a redwood ram, chiseled out of a ton-and-a-half stump, that is the campus mascot at City College.

129

The Chicago & North Western Line offered a three-act playlet on the joys of railroad travel that ended with the entire cast truckin' off stage.

Sometimes, when I feel as though that fire had taken place in my own head, sweeping away everything but a few disordered relics, I am sorry I did not keep a diary of the exposition years. I was delighted to discover while writing this book that Patti Carruthers, a friend of mine, not only kept a journal of her visits to the fair but also managed to preserve it intact through such distractions as a writing career, marriage and motherhood. Patti's diary fills a neat little scrapbook, bound in wooden covers with leather thongs and decorated with a picture of a giant cactus and the words "Golden Gate 1939 International Exposition" burned onto the front cover with a stylus. The inside pages are garnished with Heinz pickle pins, aluminum coins from the Union Pacific exhibit and other persistent, small commercial souvenirs that children cannot bear to throw away.

Patti was a tireless fair-goer and a meticulous diarist. She began her log with a preview visit three months before the Exposition opened, then gave a building-by-building report, starting, of course, with Food and Beverages. "We stayed here quite some time as free samples were given often." Like the correspondent of the *Night Hawk* Patti was enthralled by the Science Building:

— We saw many extraordinary feats of science. Such as, the wonders of plastic surgery, a television set in operation, the curing of diseases, and many other wonders too numerable to mention . . . One interesting one showed the effects of mariwahana, it was shown in a very interesting and educated way.

I am particularly grateful for Patti's succinct catalogue of exhibits she had seen.

— *Mark Twain Exhibit:* The building was advertised as free, but no one got out until you "contributed something."

— *Live Stock Pavillion:* There were only two kinds of animals, pigs and cows.

— *Coast Guard Pavillion:* Many muriels of the sea.

— *Australian Building:* The kangaroos were alive. We also saw native birds, they too were alive.

— *Model Homes:* We saw them all including the house which has an admission of ten cents. We saw this free by going in the back door.

Unfortunately, neither Patti nor I made a similar catalogue of the famous exhibit of European, American and Asian masterworks in the Hall of Fine and Decorative Arts. I regret this, because my opinions of art were as pronounced as they were uneducated. Along with Patti's views, they might illuminate the attitudes of some average young Americans at that time. It was my judgment, for example, that Botticelli's "Birth of Venus" was ridiculous — a windblown redhead, standing naked in a giant clamshell. On the other hand, I liked Salvadore Dali's surrealist landscape "Construction with Soft Beans, a Premonition of Civil War." Its title and its contents baffled me, but I figured they must be deep.

Older and better-trained critics viewed the art exhibit with a more balanced outlook. They gave it an arbitrary value of $40,000,000 and called it the greatest collection of European art ever shown in the Western Hemisphere, which it was. My mother, for one, remembers the exhibit as her initiation to fine art. Perhaps it performed the same function for thousands of other Americans who dutifully filed past Raphael's "Madonna of the Chair" and Verrocchio's bronze of David with the head of Goliath, knowing (because the gallery guide told them so) that these were masterpieces, but wondering what it was, other than antiquity, that gave immortal fame to certain objects of the past.

There was a beautiful blindness about the art exhibit. Its sponsors naturally refused to take the median taste of the American public as a criterion of what to include. They sent Dr. Walter Heil, the director of the De Young Museum, to Europe on a grand borrowing tour, and he assembled a collection that made the aircraft hangar on Treasure Island a temporary rival of the great museums of the Old World. Roland McKinney, the director for American art, selected work from 350 artists in fifty-five cities. Dorothy Wright Liebes filled a gallery of decorative arts with designs by Richard Neutra, Mies van der Rohe and their peers; and the Harvard University orientalist Langdon Warner stocked seven rooms with precious bronzes, porcelain, jade and ivory from China, Japan, Southeast Asia and the Pacific Islands.

Enticed by such treasures, the profane public remained profane. During the first six months of the Exposition, the art exhibit (adults twenty-five cents, children ten cents)grossed less than Sally Rand's Nude Ranch (adults only, twenty-five cents). Of course, there were a lot of repeaters at Sally's. When the receipts of the art exhibit finally crept ahead of the income of the Nude Ranch, the Exposition sent out news bulletins. American philistinism had been overthrown! H.L .Mencken and Sinclair Lewis were confounded! San Francisco's pretensions to culture were confirmed!

I hadn't realized so much was at stake. There had been some talk in my household about the churlishness of people who failed to take in the Old Masters, but I did not regard it as a serious problem. It seemed to me that an exposition ought to present the arts of the past out of courtesy, as a formal obeisance to historic tradition and a form of recreation for people who liked to look at pictures; but the main function of an exposition, in my opinion, was to celebrate technology, as Henry Adams had observed at Paris in 1900, when he saw the power of the Virgin of Chartres overthrown by the new force of the dynamo.

Treasure Island had been built to advertise bridges, pep up business and show off an array of up-to-date inventions —to demonstrate how sound could travel on a beam of light and color could move on a wave of sound; to exhibit houses made of plate glass and shoes made of Lucite; to unveil a model of the atom-smasher that the University of California was building in the hills of Berkeley; to dazzle the weary world with petroleum fountains, transparent telephones, voice mirrors, 50,000-watt light bulbs, television receivers and talking robots.

To me, these were commendable objectives. I believed in the benevolence of business and the extraordinary feats of science. It had not yet dawned on me — or on most other Americans, either — that technological progress exacts a price from its beneficiaries.

U.S. Steel's prophetic diorama of San Francisco in 1999 showed clustered 60-story towers in the financial district and port facilities concentrated at a single pier south of Market Street.

Like most American expositions, Treasure Island put great store by transportation. Anyone with a new conveyance to display could find a stand. Bring on the motorized dog sled, the bicycle-built-for-ten, the streamlined passenger train, the twenty-seven-millionth Ford motor car. There were innumerable vehicles to ride in: rickshaws, trikeshaws, Atlantic City bath chairs, swan boats, scooter cars, pirate galleons, giant cranes. For a dime you could circle the island in a rubber-tired tally-ho drawn by a truck with the snout of an elephant. A quarter would get you into a diving bell that visited the bottom of a tank inhabited by manta rays. A few dollars would buy a seat on Paul Mantz's Sikorsky seaplane for a twenty-minute flight above the bay.

The top in expense and celebrity were the Pan American Clipper ships, which occupied the hangar adjoining the art museum. The Clippers were graceless, heavy-bodied craft, but they were the most romantic vessels of the day, comparable in their brief glory to the first ocean-going steamships or the first trains across the continent. Thousands of spectators gathered to watch the weekly arrivals and departures at a cove on the south shore of the island. Mechanics in swimming trunks would wade out to make the ship fast while the people on shore kept respectful silence.

Pan American had begun regular flights from the Bay Area to the Orient in November, 1935. Just before the Exposition began, the company put into service five new Boeing B-314 "flying boats," replacing the older Martin Clippers. For all their ugliness, the B-314's offered unprecedented luxuries to the passengers — card tables, dining rooms, sleeping quarters — and it cost a fortune to fly in them. The fare from San Francisco to Hong Kong was well over $1,000, the equivalent of at least $5,000 today. (In 1939 you could buy a new Studebaker Champion for $660.) It took three and one-half days to make the 9,000-mile trip across the Pacific, plopping down for fuel and rest at Guam and Wake and Midway, lonely little outposts of American enterprise in the far Pacific. The passengers were millionaires and heads of state who carried draft treaties and Nobel prizes in their briefcases. To watch them boarding the Clipper was to share for an instant the high adventure of their lives. They left the Orient Express, the Blue Train and the Trans-Siberian chugging to extinction in the shadow of their wings.

I remember thinking as I watched one of the B-314 Clippers wallowing through the shallows of the cove that I, too, might some day see Wake Island or Guam. There must have been many other boys with the same thought who were surprised at how rapidly their ambitions were fulfilled.

Union pickets protested working conditions at a chain of kiosks that sold french fried potatoes and corn on the cob.

Seaplane concession, run by stunt pilot Paul Mantz, offered 20-minute rides over the island in a ten-passenger Sikorsky amphibian, a thrilling experience for thousands who had never ridden in an airplane.

VEHICLES FOR ADVENTURE

Directly or indirectly, most world expositions celebrate some achievement in the field of transportation — a railroad, subway, space flight or ship canal. Treasure Island, of course, was an occasion to show off two new bridges and a future airport and to suggest, somewhat prematurely as it turned out, that the Pacific Ocean was now a frogpond. The island's own transportation system, however, was a quiet, slow-moving, old-fashioned mixture of rickshaws, wheeled chairs and paddleboats. They were vehicles for adventure, not convenience. If you had money and courage, you could take off for a flight around the bay or across the Pacific, but most visitors to Treasure Island chose comfortable shoes, walked until their feet were tired and then hopped an Elephant Train back to the ferryboat.

Pedal-operated Swan Boats churned around the Lake of Nations, under bridges, past Oriental palaces.

A tally-ho with an elephant's head

Balloon-tired passenger trains, decorated with the trappings of Indian elephants, shuttled between the parking lot and the main gate, rounded the Lake of Nations, prowled the fringes of the amusement zone.

When you examined them closely, the celebrated Elephant Trains turned out to be merely strong passenger cars towing strings of tally-ho wagons with colored awnings and open seats.

136

It was the paisley howdah over the driver's seat, the elephant snout superimposed on the engine hood, that gave them a peculiar charm and marked them as close relations of the huge, cubist elephants that lorded over the western walls. As such, the Elephant Trains were products of Pacific Basin Style — perhaps its most enduring souvenir, destined to grace a hundred fairgrounds, zoos and parking lots to the present day.

Follow that rickshaw!

An enterprising businessman named Toy Mon Sing had the jinrikisha concession in 1939, and it was, so to speak, tough sledding. Americans had "feelings" about rickshaws. Rickshaws were pulled by starving coolies who lived on one bowl of rice a day, and they were ridden by geisha girls and implacable Fu Manchu-types with wispy black mustaches and six-inch fingernails. Whatever the reality, Americans felt uncomfortable in rickshaws, as if they were doing something immoral, publicly flaunting the Bill of Rights.

The push chairs, on the other hand, were propelled by strong, well-fed fraternity men from Cal and Stanford. Who could resist helping a struggling Deke to earn his daily bowl of rice?

Inexhaustible Zoe Dell Lantis, flying U.S. colors,
won a rigged race to promote the sagging jinrikisha business.

A photo of cowboy star Tom Mix in a rickshaw caused an efflorescence of dreadful West-meets-East caption writing.

Two-seater rolling chairs, at 50 cents a person for a half-hour ride, seemed expensive to many fair-goers.

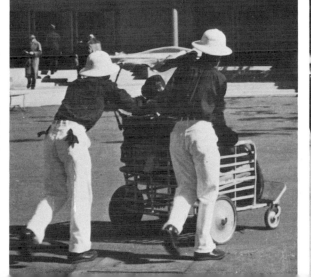

The immortal clippers

The Hall of Air Transportation was the simplest, most successful exhibit on Treasure Island — a hangar, where transpacific planes were fueled and groomed for flights to the Orient. Pan American Airways had begun regular flights from the Bay Area late in 1935. In 1939, as if to honor the fair, Pan Am put five new Boeing-314 Flying Boats into service, basing them at Treasure Island. To watch the China Clippers landing in San Francisco Bay was to see evidence that the unity of the Pacific was more than an architectural theme.

Up to now, I have treated the Exposition as a single event, which is the way most people think of it. Actually, it was two fairs, in two successive years, and the second differed considerably from the first.

The 1939 fair, despite its fragile beauty and its air of self-confidence, was an awful flop. (I find it painful to admit this, because I was ignorant of the truth at the time. It is like learning that a book you cherished as a child is regarded by educated people as vulgar trash.) The promoters had grossly over-estimated the size and spending habits of the audience. They were expecting about 2,500,000 customers each month. Less than half that number showed up during each of the first two months. Thousands entered at a reduced rate on season tickets, free passes or special-day discounts. Thousands of others were children, like Patti Carruthers and me, who got in for a dime, ate a bag lunch in the Court of Pacifica, free-loaded at the Junket exhibit and sneaked in the back door of the model homes.

The concessionaires in the Gayway were furious. They hounded Leland Cutler to reduce rents, lower gate charges and bring in more zippy attractions.

"Every time I went out on the grounds to look things over or get a little relaxation, I would be besieged by well-meaning people who wanted to tell me how to run the show, and I would have to take refuge in my office again," Cutler recalled in his memoirs. "Looking back, that part is a cross between a nightmare and a kaleidoscope."

At the end of the first month, the Exposition cut its payroll from 12,000 employees to about 7,000. Thirty cashiers lost their jobs one day and twenty-two the next. On weekdays the employees on the island sometimes outnumbered the paying customers.

A writer named Phil Hamilton, who did not go along with the parochial loyalty of the *Night Hawk* and other Bay Area papers, dug out the facts. *The American Mercury* published his report in June, 1939. It was called "San Francisco, A Dying City." Senior members of the Chamof Commerce still turn gray in the jowls at the thought of it.

Barbara Dean (Miss U.S.A.) Lila Deanne (Miss Exposition) and Marshall Dill (Mister President, 1940) opened the second year with a ribbon-snipping.

After reviewing in excruciating detail the history of disputes between labor and management on the San Francisco waterfront, Hamilton contrasted the expectations of the Exposition with its realizations.

"From an economic standpoint," he wrote, "the best that can be said for the fair is that it has furnished employment for a considerable number of people who would otherwise be on WPA. Instead of being the build-up for a super-colossal and altogether stupendous Gold Rush Centennial in '49, the present fiasco has a much better chance of being, for Californians, the fair to end fairs." (He was right.)

Naturally, this publication led to a general casting of blame and aspersions, and the board of directors fired the general manager, Harris Connick. It was remembered to Connick's disfavor that he had had some sort of prolonged dispute with Sally Rand about whether she should have an exclusive franchise on nude shows, and whether the girls at the Ranch ought to wear bras, and somebody said it all showed that Connick was a square and didn't know how to attract the type of show that people wanted to see twice. Phil Patchin, a vice-president of the Standard Oil Company of California, which had a large investment in the Exposition, became the acting manager.

Before long the directors were able to enlist Dr. Charles Henry Strub to take Connick's place. Dr. Strub was the operator of a chain of dental offices and of the Santa Anita race track, among other things, and he brought along some bouncy racecourse promoters to liven up the island. They soon got rid of Edwin Franko Goldman's brass band and signed up Benny Goodman and Eddie Duchin. Summer was coming in. The crowds improved.

"Business is really looking up," Kevin Wallace reported, "and by that we DON'T mean lying on its back." (Everyone was feeling defensive.)

By midsummer, however, it was obvious that even Dr. Strub and Benny Goodman could not make a world's fair profitable. The New York Fair admitted to being in worse shape than Treasure Island. Grover Whalen had to cut prices, fire employees, eliminate fireworks and make the humiliating confession that he had lied about attendance. (He had more than doubled the first day's official count.)

The 1939 Pageant of the Pacific, therefore, closed in October, six weeks early and $4,166,000 in debt. (New York lost $23,982,000 and defaulted on its debentures.) About two-thirds of the first-year creditors accepted twenty cents on the dollar and wrote off the Exposition as a loss. The remainder chose to hang on for a second year in hope of doing better. A second fair, a Fair in Forty, was bound to make a comeback: it would have a shorter season, lower admission prices, louder band concerts. The flowers would be brighter, the lights lighter, the nudes nakeder. If only *half* the people in the Bay Area would come to Treasure Island just *four* times . . .

The directors chose a new president, Marshall Dill, a perennially active citizen who had just finished a term as president of the Chamber

COBB'S *Famous* CHICKEN HOUSE ¡ THE ONLY ORIGINAL CHICKEN HOUSE ON THE FAIR GROUNDS, TREASURE ISLAND, SAN FRANCISCO, CALIFORNIA

of Commerce, and Treasure Island got a new phone number, FAir-grounds 1940.

The Forty Fair opened while the German army was pushing through the valley of the Somme toward Paris. I know this because I checked back in the newspapers. The headlines gave me a feeling of cold emptiness, and I could not read the story.

A few days after the opening, while ribbons were still on the turn-stiles, Belgium surrendered. The remnants of the allied army escaped from Dunkirk in thousands of small boats that crossed the channel from England. On June 10 ("Coolidge Quartet Day") Norway surrendered. The Norwegians had an exhibit at the fair — not the cosy log ski hut they had displayed in 1939, roofed with turf and stocked with cumin cheese and kippered herrings, but a small building that had been set up the previous year by New Zealand, a Maori meeting-house with ex-aggerated gables. Norwegians in the United States sent wood carvings and hand-knit sweaters to put on display, and the pavilion served as an office for Norwegian war relief.

It was a different fair. Everything was freshly painted. The paintings from the Uffizi and the other European galleries were gone, and Diego Rivera had come up from Mexico to work on a mural in the Hall of Fine Arts. The French and Italian pavilions were closed.

Still, I cannot keep the two years straight. They melt together in the Treasure Island of my mind as they have done throughout this book—one fair, indivisible, occupying a single territory in my personal warp of time and space, detailed but incomplete, in an annoying, transubstantial way.

I suppose it is merely a demonstration of the fallibility of memory, the way the dates and names have faded while certain flavors and aromas remain as palpable to me as the green pickle pin I keep in a stud box on my dresser. There is, for example, a certain elusive blend of salt air and fuel oil, doughnuts and old newspapers, that is the smell of the ferry boats — it makes me dangerously sentimental. Another fragrance, na-tive to the island, is composed of french fries, corn on the cob and cotton candy, delicately seasoned with seagull droppings. (Do not confuse this with the ordinary smell of country fairs, which is mostly horse manure.) The french-fry-corn-on-the-cob aroma used to swirl around the fringes of the Gayway on summer mornings, making the pickets lift their heads and grip the handles of their signs. (According to the pickets, the french fry and corn on the cob stands were unfair to labor.)

Leland Cutler and friends gave a classic demonstration of the Pacific Basin Smile.

Most of the Treasure Island foods were undistinguished — beef sandwiches, hot dogs and paper cups of Orange Crush — but a few exceptions linger in my mental cupboard. Not fancy exceptions from the Argentine Pavilion or the Café Lafayette — I never went to those expensive places, or, if I did, I quickly digested the memory — but rather Scottish scones, split open and drizzled with butter and raspberry jam; hot cocoa and Mayflower doughnuts; and tiny Dutch pancakes called *poffertjies*, sprinkled with powdered sugar.

I have a friend who associates the very name Treasure Island with chicken and mushroom luncheons where novelists spoke about The Future of California Literature. Another remembers confronting an Indonesian *rijsttafel* for the first time in some corner of the island. At a kiosk near the National Cash Register I bought the worst tuna sandwich I ever tasted. John Blayney and I decided the tuna must have come over direct from Tunisia on a camel, and we worked ourselves into a laughing fit, making up alliterative slogans for the terrible tasting Tunisian tuna industry. Modern children do not get into laughing fits over such thin material, and it is all to the good.

I am afraid this reconstruction of Treasure Island has been cluttered with many small shards of trivial memory. Odors, sounds and laughing fits stay with me like the Union Pacific coins glued into Patti Carruthers's diary. When I try to recall the Gayway ("Forty Acres of Fun"), my train of thought runs off the track, and I think instead of a poor, puffy, blue-lipped creature in Ripley's Believe-It-or-Not Odditorium who called herself (or allowed herself to be called) "The Mule-Faced Woman," or of an armless man, same institution, who threw butcher knives at his wife with his feet, or of a souvenir (where have they gone?) called Movie-of-U — not really a movie, of course, but a triple exposure, three facial expressions, with a layer of pin-striped celluloid over it that made the face-of-U twitch through a three-phase cycle of tics and grimaces when you turned a crank.

The Gayway was a grand atelier of useless artifacts. Most of them, fortunately, have disappeared as painlessly as Movies-of-U. But the Gayway was odorous and highly-seasoned and the flavor comes back.

Every adult I knew said the Gayway was garish, cheap, and boring. As usual, they were right. On their advice, I treated the Gayway as confection that would rot your teeth. I went there at the end of the day, after an appropriate number of constructive exhibits, and blew the rest of my money on the Tilt-a-Whirl and dodger cars.

On a clear day you could see
12,000 cars in the Treasure
Island parking lot.

But I loved it slavishly. One by one, the pitchmen overpowered me. I bought a Hum-a-Tune from a man in a Chico Marx hat. I sat for my portrait by a girl who worked at an easel in a pit adjoining the sand sculpture of Christ in the Garden. I let Lady Alice read my mind.

As every adult I knew had warned me, the Hum-a-Tune that played melodiously for the man in the Chico Marx hat played not at all for me. The portrait had curly hair and blue eyes. Lady Alice read me wrong. I have no regrets.

In the parlance of the Old South, a Gayway is a redlight district. Neither the concessionaires nor the customers seemed to know about this. It might have given them all hope. In those days, few Americans knew the homosexual connotations of "gay," either. The name was only a winning entry in a contest. Like the zone, it promised more than it gave.

An atmosphere of desperation pervaded the Gayway. I presume it was a natural reaction to going broke, which most of the concessionaires were doing. When the barkers cried "Last chance!" they meant it. Grind Shows and Villages disappeared overnight, leaving bills and padlocks.

Most of them left without the benefit of my patronage. They lost a sympathetic customer. I would have preferred Virgins in Cellophane or DuBarry on the Half Shell to Ripley's Odditorium, but our society, then as now, had peculiar standards of obscenity.

Every week or so I was rebuffed at the ticket window of "Elysium," wherein Miss Kathryn Gay performed Dances from the World of Tomorrow, "where fashion is unknown and clothing a Thing of the Past." Every week or so they turned me away at Sally Rand's.

If the fair had lasted a few more years, I would have been of age to safely see for myself the World of Tomorrow and the volleyball courts of Paradise, where acrobatic cowgirls in boots, sombreros and holster belts cavorted behind glass in twenty-minute shifts. That much I do regret.

148

FREAKS, GIRLS
AND DIVING-BELLS

The fastest way to irritate a person of good taste during the Exposition years was to suggest that the Gayway reflected the cultural standards of the Bay Area. What it reflected, you would immediately learn, was the vulgar enterprise of certain concessionaires who had installed eighty-two midgets in cowboy outfits in a miniature western village; a diving bell in a tank of fish; a Scottish village, complete with But-and-Ben cottages, gin-and-ginger beer and a wandering goose; an automobile racetrack for monkeys; an exhibit of Chinese acrobats; a movie of nudists playing volleyball; and a whole avenue of shooting galleries, roller coasters, Hindu rope tricks, Roll-O-Planes, reptile pits and flea circuses — all on the theory that anything people liked had a place at a world's fair.

It turned out that both the people of good taste and the vulgar concessionaires were wrong. Some people liked the Gayway, some people didn't, and about two-thirds of the shows went broke.

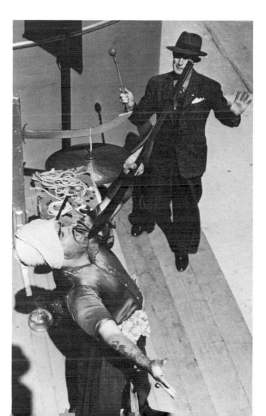

In the second year the Gayway was festooned with used-car
pennants and offered more penny arcades and carnival rides.

Monkey auto racers sustained a lively numbers game.

At the Artists & Models Studio you could
sketch, photograph or ogle nude models.

The Giant Crane,
a Swiss import,
treated several
dozen passengers
to a windy view
from the top of
the Y-beam.

Premature babies in glass cases drew curious crowds. The barkers
and ticket takers wore surgical gowns and spoke in hushed voices.

Sally's organic ranch

Sally Rand's Nude Ranch bore the name of the most celebrated performer at the 1932 Chicago World's Fair, but, instead of Sally and her feather boa, the Ranch unveiled forty-seven sporty young women who pitched horseshoes, swung lariats, rode burros and played badminton in boots and G-strings while the audience peeked through plate glass panels. Twenty girls at a time cavorted on stage in a continuous performance from 1 P.M. to 2 A.M. They changed shifts every forty minutes, spent their twenty-minute breaks reading, writing letters and taking showers. In the first week of the Fair, 65,000 people paid twenty-five cents each to see the athletics.

Stella, the sensation of the 1915 Exposition, had a short run at Treasure Island. Word got around that she was only a painting of a reclining nude with a machine-operated bosom that rocked and heaved, and that kind of fetish wasn't worth a dime in 1939.

154 *The art that H.L. Mencken called "ecdysiasm" flourished in the Gayway.*
Mencken's monstrous euphemism came from the Greek word for molting.

An art form
for every taste

According to F.M. Sandusky, the director of concessions, the Gayway was as raunchy as Panama City. Still, clergymen and women's clubs failed to attack the zone on moral grounds, so Sandusky had to do it for them. He announced that sex shows would be "bottled up" in a walled compound so that "mothers and children will be able to travel the Gayway in safety."

"Anyone passing through that gate will know in advance what he's going to get," Sandusky promised. The mothers and children of the Bay Area were eternally grateful.

A Hum-a-Tune was a kazoo made of two aluminum disks. At 25 cents the profit was fantastic, sweetheart, absolutely fantastic.

Quick-sketch artists shared a dugout with Claude Bell of Atlantic City, who was into sand sculpture. Claude used sharp sand (as opposed to round sand) because it stuck together better, but he kept his source a secret.

155

An aerial stunt show at the north end of the Gayway had a man shot from a cannon, high-wire walkers and the scariest, most windblown balancing act anyone ever saw.

Before we expected it, the day came to close the gates and turn out the lights for the last time. It was a sad occasion, especially for those who had drawn subsistence from the fair — the men who guessed your weight, the photographers who took your picture, the woman who pressed 200 shirts a day with a General Electric iron. It was sad for the rest of us, too, who had found refreshment on Treasure Island.

When the final bills had been paid and the last scrap of salvage sold, it would be recorded that the Golden Gate International Exposition, like many others before and since, had lost money. The staff compiled a final report, cleaned out the files and drifted away. The administrative office on Bush Street became the headquarters of San Francisco's public welfare department.

The directors advertised the plaster palaces for demolition. The newspapers showed pictures of the Tower of the Sun collapsing and the Japanese Pavilion in flames. After the flounciest structures were gone, the navy asked for the rest, and San Francisco handed over the island as a temporary base.

The navy transformed the Hall of Western States into a barracks and the Food and Beverages Building into the largest mess hall on earth: 7,000 meals an hour, s-o-s and peanut butter soup. Navy recruits took classes in engineering aboard the riverboat *Delta Queen*, which had ferried patrons to the Exposition. The model home, landscaped by the California Nursery Company and vulnerable from the rear, became an officers' club.

Hundreds of thousands of men passed through the receiving center during World War II. Stripped of towers and flowering trees, Treasure Island was a damp gray bivouac, associated in the minds of its transient inhabitants with cat fever and head colds, radar training and embarcation for the zone of combat.

The streets followed pathways we had traveled in rickshaws and elephant trains, but the alluring names that Clyde Vandeburg and Ted Huggins had made up vanished from the landscape. The Avenue of Palms became Avenue A. California Street turned into Second Street, and the Concourse of Commonwealths deflated to Avenue M. The exotic Passiflora Street, the mellifluous Avenue of Olives were gone forever. Only the name of Stevenson's island remained to cast a shadow of the past, a sentimental civilian imprint on the rectangle of tidal mud.

When the war was over, San Francisco lost its ambition to build an airport in the center of the bay. Treasure Island had turned out to be too small, too close to the bridge and altogether too convenient to the upstart town that called itself "Treasure Island's Mainland." The navy offered to trade some government property adjoining Mills Field in San Mateo County for the deed to the island, and the city accepted. Out of the transaction came the San Francisco International Airport and the Treasure Island Naval Station.

As a harbinger of style, the Exposition had totally failed. It left no permanent monuments — no Eiffel Tower, no Prater Ferris Wheel, no Palace of Fine Arts. It set no artistic or architectural trends. The times were against it; nobody was building or designing anything but military camps. The very concept of a Pacific Basin style began to sound like an ironic mockery. The Pacific Basin was not a cultural unity — it was a theater of war. The world was too distracted to support a bright new bubble of creative energy. If this generation was to make a mark on history, it would have to do so in another way, by fighting a war we had been hoping to avoid.

With nervous haste we tore the towers down and scattered the statues. Diego Rivera's mural went into the library at San Francisco City College. Robert Howard's "Whales" showed up at the Aquarium. The Yerba Buena Club auctioned its upholstered chairs.

Recently, a mist has drifted around the memory of Treasure Island, cloaking those Cambodian towers in the tint of a new discovery. Many things that seemed insipid or pretentious a few years ago now strike us as naive and tender, the honorable products of a small provincial city that was just not ready to be Florence; and the fair stands scrutiny once again as the symbolic climax of an era that was neither proud nor happy, yet infinitely sweet compared to that which lay immediately ahead.

A RAINBOW BY NIGHT

Treasure Island spent $1,500,000 for night lighting. Blue spotlights, pink fluorescent tubes and ultraviolet "black lights" hid in every shrub and nestled in the creases of the Cambodian Towers. Flecks of iridescent mica scintillated in stuccoed walls. Fountains changed color; statues glowed with eerie phosphorescence; and the great Prayer Curtain, shivering behind the statue of Pacifica, faded perceptibly from dark blue to pale apricot.

It was the tour de force of the Exposition — an expensive, flamboyant burst of color in a world of night air raids and blacked-out cities, as joyful as a show of fireworks on Independence Day, and as ephemeral.

The Court of the Moon, bathed in mauve and blue, was the public favorite.
The color scheme remained unchanged the second year, when General Electric
lighting consultants gave all other buildings brighter, brasher hues —

Fireworks displays were executed by a pyrotechnician named
Roland Oliver, who specialized in yellow octopus scatterbombs,
red waterfire, pink elephants and Mickey Mouse levitations.

The night show on General Electric Day ended with a radio broadcast transmitted on a beam of light from the top of the Tower of the Sun to a receiver in the Temple Compound.

Gayway lights were glaring white and unsophisticated, made the zone seem friendlier by night than by day.

A fan of super spotlights near the South Pool could be seen for dozens of miles on a night of special events.

The Fountain of Life in the Court of Flowers had jets of white water surrounded by shrubbery lit by mercury vapor lamps.

Mural "The Peacemakers," by Margaret, Helen and Esther Bruton, seemed to spring out in deep relief when flooded by pure white spotlights. The work was actually a low relief and painting, showing Occidental and Oriental figures meeting at the feet of Buddha in a setting that included the Great Wall of China, an Aztec pyramid, the Bay Bridge and a sample of Pacific Basin architecture.

On the final night, September 29, 1940, several thousand guests stayed on, by invitation, after the public gates were locked. Huddled together in the wind, they stared around them in anticipation and dismay. For several months they had sensed a growing guilt about the Exposition. Fun was out of fashion. It was time now to end the foolishness and turn to other things.

Yet they longed to save some trace of Treasure Island in their minds, some mark of faith in the endurance of beauty, the recurrence of joy, the consolation of laughter. The fair had been a sedative, of course, a tranquilizer for a frightened generation; we had understood this and accepted it with gratitude. We welcomed our brief oblivion and clung to our illusive innocence as long as the spell would last. In a world consumed by rage, there would be no further respites, no more innocent islands.

The columnist Herb Caen, who mirrors the vagrant moods of his beloved city, recalled years later the desolation of that moment when the island flickered into darkness — "and you knew, suddenly, that an era had ended for a generation that would never be young again."

Marshall Dill made the last speech.

"Yesterday's bright vision of Treasure Island today becomes an enduring memory that will hearten us in the toilsome times that unhappily now are in prospect. Now we must give up our silver trumpet for one of brass. For the past four months we have been joyously tending our garden while all around us the world has been bent on destruction. I like to think that all the peaceful legions that have trouped through this fair have had their spiritual wells deepened and are now prepared for whatever Fate may have in store . . . 'The feast is over and the lamps expire.' "

The lights went out. The exposition years were over. We turned to other things.

On the final night of the Exposition a photographer on Cragmont Avenue in the Berkeley Hills made this time exposure of Treasure Island illuminated for the last time.

Acknowledgements

The author is indebted to many persons, institutions and business firms for giving time, disclosing memories and lending photographs and souvenirs for this restoration project. Two historical archives — that of the San Francisco Public Library and that of the California Historical Society — were especially rich in material and generous in assistance, and the incomparable Bancroft Library of the University of California at Berkeley again proved that it is an indispensable resource for any study of California, even of recent history.

Among those who obligingly helped to dig out the pictures were Frances Buxton of the California Room, Oakland Public Library; Carney Campion and Norma Flannery of the Redwood Empire Association; Guy Carruthers, Standard Oil Company of California; Theodore Bache, Pan American World Airways; Stan August, Bill Robertson and George Kraus, Southern Pacific Company; Virginia Dennison, Alameda-Contra Costa Transit District; Carolyn T. Wharton and Cecilia LeBoeuf, Army Corps of Engineers; Peter A. Evans and Lee L. Burtis, California Historical Society; Susan Burns and Theresa Heyman, Oakland Museum; John Barr Tompkins, Bancroft Library; James Kantor, University of California Archives; Barney Barnett, San Francisco Photography Center; Gladys Hansen, Special Collections Department, San Francisco Public Library; Larry Lieurance, San Francisco *Examiner*; Anna Parker, San Francisco *Chronicle*; Katherine Titsworth, Pacific Telephone Company; and Fred Gass, U.S. Naval Station, Treasure Island.

The California section of the State Library, Sacramento, the National Archives, the Library of Congress, the United States Steel Corporation, the General Electric Company, the Wells Fargo Bank History Room, the Italian-Swiss Colony Winery and the Dallas Museum of Fine Arts also provided valuable assistance.

Above all, thanks are due to those who shared their private collections and personal memories of Treasure Island: Clyde Vandeburg, Zoe Dell Nutter, Ken Wilson, Barney Gould, Ted Huggins, Kevin Wallace, Patti Carruthers, Tom Watkins, Marilyn and Bill Bronson, Luella Sawyer, Ray Moulin and Paul Johnson.

Two press agents of the Golden Gate International Exposition, Jack James and Earle Weller, recorded their remembrances in a postmortem volume (*Treasure Island*, "*The Magic City*," San Francisco, 1941) which is as close as anyone came to writing an official history. It was a basic source for my book, as were the two *Official Guide Books* (1939 and 1940) published in San Francisco by the H.S. Crocker Company. George Creel's autobiography (*Rebel at Large*, New York, 1947), and Leland Cutler's memoirs (*America Is Good to a Country Boy*, Stanford, 1954), opened the doors of forgotten financial conferences and vanished administrative offices.

Picture credits

Full thanks are due to many individuals and organizations for their permission to make use of their photographs. Below are listed, page-by-page, the photographic credits of this book. The key to abbreviations appears below the credits.

Title page–Moulin; 6–Moulin; 10–SFPL; 11–CHS; 12–(tl)Bancroft, (tr,m)SP; 13–(2)SP; 14–(4)SP; 15–(tl, bl)Bancroft, (r)Moulin; 16–(tl)Wide World, (3)DLOM; 17–(t)SFPL, (3) DLOM; 18–(t)SFPL, (2)Bancroft; 19–Bancroft; 20–(tl, bl)Bancroft, (r)SFPL; 21–(bl) SFPL, (5)Bancroft; 22–Bancroft; 23–(t)CSL, (b)CHS; 24–(t)Bancroft, (l)CHS; 25-26-27–CHS; 28–(l)Bancroft, (r)OPL; 29–(3)CHS; 30-31-32–CHS; 33–(t)Chronicle, (2)SFPL; 34 –OPL; 37-38-39–SFPL; 41–UC; 42 & 45–CHS; 46–SFPL; 47–Bancroft; 48 (3)ACE; 49-50–SFPL; 51–(tr)CHS, (2)SFPL; 52–CHS; 53–Bancroft; 54–CHS; 55-56-57-58–SFPL; 59–LC; 60–(7)Nutter; 61–(br)CHS, (2)SFPL; 62–Gould; 63–SFPL; 65 & 67–Bancroft; 68–CHS; 69–SFPL; 70–(t)Bancroft; 70(b)-71(2) –Chronicle; 72–(t)Examiner, (b)SFPL; 73–Chronicle; 74-75–SFPL; 76–(t)SP, (b)Moulin; 77–(t)CHS, (b)SFPL; 78–Examiner; 79–(t2) Bancroft, (bl)SP, (br)SO; 80 CHS; 81–SFPL; 82–Bancroft; 83–SFPL; 84–SP; 85–SFPL; 86 –(l)Moulin, (tr)Sawyer, (br)SFPL; 87–USNS; 88–(2)UC; 89–(l2)PacTel, (r)SFPL; 90–(2)UC; 92-93–Bancroft; 94–CHS; 95–LC; 96–(t) SFPL, (b)CHS; 97–(2)SFPL; 98–(t)LC, (b) CHS; 99–(t)CHS, (b2)Bancroft; 100–CHS; 101–(t)LC, (4)SFPL; 102–(t)REA, (2)SFPL; 103–(t)Chronicle, (b)SFPL; 104–SFPL; 105–(t)SFPL, (b)CHS; 106–Chronicle; 107–OM; 108–Chronicle; 109–Bancroft; 110–Wells; 111–OM; 112–SP; 113–CHS; 114–(bl)CHS, (t, br)SFPL; 115–CHS; 116–Chronicle; 117–(3)Gould; 118 & 120–Bancroft; 121–Wells; 122–(tl)Moulin, (bl)USS, (tr, br)REA; 123–(bl)SO, (m, br)Bancroft; 124–(2)SFPL; 125–(t)Chronicle, (b)SFPL; 126–(2)PTT; 127–(bl) PTT, (tr)SO, (br)REA; 128-129–Call; 130–SFPL; 131–Sawyer; 132–USS; 133–Sawyer; 134–CHS; 135–SFPL; 136–(l)SP, (r)Sawyer; 137–(t)Sawyer, (b)CHS; 138–Examiner; 139–(t)National Archives, (b2)CHS; 140-141-142 (t)–PAA; 142–(b)Bancroft; 143–Chronicle; 144–(2)CHS; 145–Chronicle; 146–(t)Bancroft, (b)SFPL; 147–(t)Moulin, (b)CHS; 148–SFPL; 149–Moulin; 150–(t)CHS, (b)Chronicle; 151–(tl)Bancroft, (2)Moulin; 152–(l)Moulin, (r) SFPL; 153–(t)SFPL, (b)Chronicle; 154–Moulin; 155–(2)SFPL, 156–Call; 157–CHS, 158-159–SFPL; 160–SFPL; 161–Bancroft; 162–SFPL; 163–CHS; 164–SFPL; 165–(t)General Electric, (m)Moulin, (b)Chronicle; 166–SFPL; 167–(2)CHS; 169–CHS.

The Key

ACE: Department of the Army, Corps of Engineers, San Francisco; Bancroft: Bancroft Library, University of California, Berkeley; Chronicle: The *San Francisco Chronicle*; CHS: The California Historical Society; CSL: California Section, California State Library, Sacramento; Call: The *San Francisco Call-Bulletin*, from the Bancroft Library; DLOM: Dorothea Lange Collection, The Oakland Museum; Examiner: The *San Francisco Examiner*; Gould: Barney Gould; LC: Library of Congress; Moulin: Gabriel Moulin Studios, San Francisco; Nutter: Zoe Dell Lantis Nutter; OM: The Oakland Museum; OPL: The California Room, Oakland Public Library; PAA: Pan American World Airways, San Francisco; PacTel: The Pacific Telephone & Telegraph Company, San Francisco; REA: The Redwood Empire Association; Sawyer: Luella Sawyer; SFPL: Special Collections, San Francisco Public Library; SO: The Standard Oil Company of California; SP: The Southern Pacific Transportation Company; UC: Environmental Design Library, University of California, Berkeley; USNS: United States Naval Station, Treasure Island; USS: The United States Steel Corp., San Francisco; Wells: The Wells Fargo Bank History Room, San Francisco; Wide World: Wide World Photos, New York

Index

(Photographs are denoted by italicized page references)